The Requirement of Grief

The Requirement of Grief

A Memoir

Danielle Ariano

atmosphere press

Table of Contents

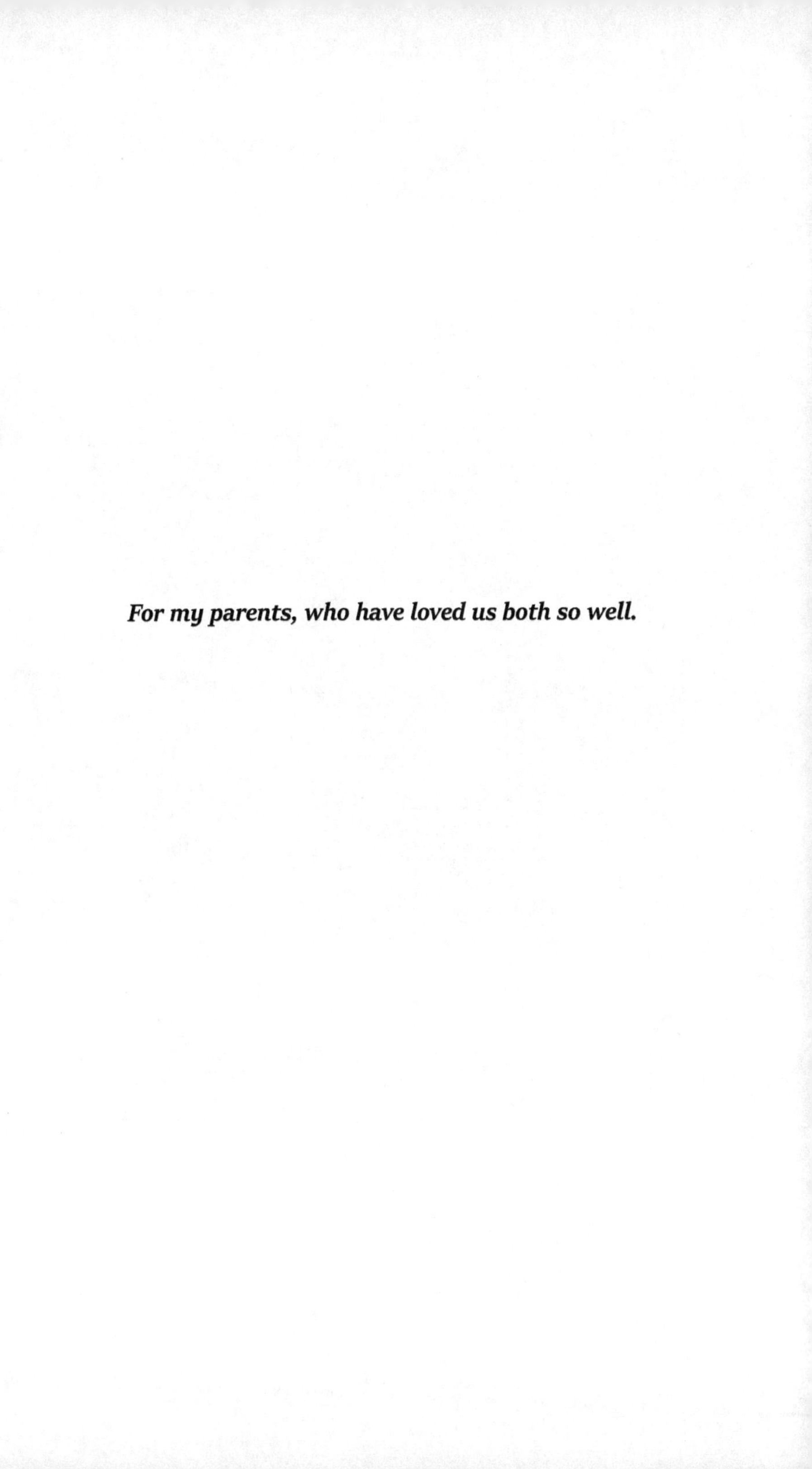

For my parents, who have loved us both so well.

To understand is to forgive, even oneself.
– Alexander Chase

The Weekend

SHE RUMMAGES THROUGH the freezer until she finds some ravioli from the Italian place that her mother loves. *Perfect,* she thinks as she fills a pot with water and sets it on the stove. She's not much of a cook, but she can handle ravioli. Her parents are leaving tomorrow for a three-day trip to Florida. When they return, she will be dead.

Does she already know in this moment? As she pulls frozen pasta from the freezer, does she know? Is it all mapped out? She has tried to end her life so many times before—thirteen— so does she feel more determined this time? Is she sure?

In a large bowl, she tosses the washed lettuce, then throws croutons and cheese on top. *What else?* she wonders as she checks the water and notes that the bottom of the pot is covered with tiny bubbles that have begun to break off and float to the top.

This has to be special. Her parents' 46th wedding anniversary is in three days. She googles how to make Cosmopolitans and then runs to retrieve a couple of bottles from the liquor cabinet.

Does she intend to share their anniversary? Does she consider the fact that they will not find her until they return home on May 23rd, the actual day they got married forty-six years ago? Is this an act of adoration or spite? Or is it just desperation?

"Shit, shit, shit," she says when she returns to find the water boiling over. After rushing to turn the burner down, she throws the ravioli into the pot and then does her best to estimate each ingredient for the Cosmos.

Her parents will want coffee afterward, but coffee is too plain for such an occasion, so she goes into the basement and digs through the boxes from her old apartment until she finds her cappuccino maker. These boxes have been here collecting dust for two and a half years, ever since she became unable to live on her own. She hopes that this will be a good memory for them to hold onto after she is gone. An image of her parents' faces twisted in pain flashes through her mind. Stop, she tells herself. If anything will deter her, it's thinking of her parents' pain, but she knows that in the long run, they'll be happier without her. Upstairs a timer starts beeping, and she hurries to turn it off.

In the kitchen, she focuses on getting the cappuccino machine set up by screwing the steamer arm in place and plugging the maker into the outlet to check that it still works. She must not think of her parents this way again. She runs some water through the machine to clean it out.

As she sets the table, the voices begin.

Or perhaps the voices have been talking to her the entire time and she blocked them out in order to get as far as she has with the dinner. Perhaps every moment is a struggle?

"The T.V. isn't on," they tell her, "but they're still watching you."

Sometimes she can turn down their volume by drinking a lot, but she seems to have less and less control over them lately. They sow worry into every moment. They're suspicious of everything and everyone. She runs over to the T.V. and unplugs it, then unhooks the cable box.

"You better check your medicine. You know someone keeps stealing it."

She goes upstairs to the safe where her parents have been keeping her medications and sees that it's still locked. The light on the Wi-Fi router glows ominously, so she pulls the cord from the wall socket.

In a recent journal entry, she tracked the voices' volume and made notes on what helped to quiet them. A science experiment. Two glasses of wine, one Ativan: still laughing. Three more Ativan and another glass of wine: quieter.

"Hello? Alexis?" her mother calls up to her. "I'm home."

Her mom does this each day when she gets back from work. Sometimes her mom's voice calling up the stairs is what wakes her at 5:30 p.m. On those days, her mother gets angry and no matter what she does to placate her—set the table, help with the dishes—it makes no difference.

She releases the black power cord from her fingers. Her father will be upset that he has to reprogram the T.V., but she's protecting them, so she'll just have to deal with his anger.

"Hey Mom," she calls back, rushing down the steps. "I'm making you and Dad dinner for your anniversary," she says tentatively, unsure how her mother will react. Her mom's eyebrows go up.

"Oh?" She smiles.

Relief floods through her body. "Yeah."

When her father comes home, he gives a crooked half-smile at the news of the dinner as he rips open a bill from the mail pile. They both sit down at the table, as she has instructed them. She lights the candles that she dug out of the drawer and then delivers each of them a plate of ravioli.

"Oh, I almost forgot," she says, grabbing the two Cosmos off the counter.

"Woo woo, fan-cy," her mom says with a smile, taking a sip.

"What a treat," her father says.

"You're not eating with us?" her mother asks her as she walks out of the kitchen.

"No," she says firmly, waving her hand to dismiss the idea. She retreats to the couch in the living room. "It's your anniversary dinner."

She thinks of the fact that tomorrow her parents will be sitting in beach chairs, digging their toes into the sand. She imagines a whole scenario in which they go out to a nice dinner: her father orders a Manhattan straight up and gives the cherry to her mom; her mother orders a glass of Chardonnay and then spoons ice cubes out of her water, dropping them into her wine; the two of them clink glasses and toast to "relaxing," which she believes to be their coded way of expressing relief over being away from her for a few days.

Her parents are a marvel to her, loving each other for almost half a century. She's been in love many times. Jason, James, Patrick, Joe, Billy, Matt. None of those loves were like the love her parents have. Jason and Patrick hit her. Matt and Billy stole from her, which hurt more than the physical abuse. The stealing was so unnecessary. She would've given them anything they'd asked for, so when they stole things it felt as though she'd failed to convince them of that. She loved most of her partners more than they loved her. To each of these men, she surrendered herself.

Only Terry and Chris had been different. Both of them had adored her, but she never loved them back, not really. She tried. God, had she tried, but the more they fawned over her, the more punishing she acted toward them in this way that made her feel unrecognizable to herself. By nature she was not a cruel person, but she couldn't stand to hear them tell her how perfect she was. She was more comfortable with the insults the other men hurled her way.

"Well, that was delicious, thank you very much," she hears her father say. She scrambles into the kitchen to grab the plates off the table. Her father has barely touched his drink, and she fixates on how much liquid is left in his glass, taking it as a rejection.

"One more surprise," she says proudly as she pulls a towel off of the cappuccino maker. "Ta-da!" Her parents smile at one another and shake their heads in wonder as she gets to work steaming the milk.

THE NEXT MORNING she wakes early and feels so light that she decides to cook her parents breakfast. *Soon this will all be over*, she thinks, feeling buoyed, almost giddy, which is a feeling she hasn't experienced in so long. If anything was going to raise a red flag for her parents, it would be this breakfast. She's not a morning person, and she already cooked them dinner last night.

But if they're suspicious, they do not say anything. They've lived with the possibility of her suicide for so many years that the alarm bells have to be blaring in order to register.

Her father brings the luggage to the car. In an alternate life, she would be driving them to the airport. In an alternate life, she'd have her own car, she'd be able to drive, she'd have a job—but instead she's a forty-two-year-old woman living with her parents.

She walks them to the door, hugs her father. "Bring me back some seashells," she says.

She turns to her mother, who always looks so put together, with her carefully styled blonde hair and the prettiest blue eyes. She wraps her arms around her mom's shoulders and has to resist the urge to squeeze too tight. "Have a good time," she says.

"Don't forget to call your doctor," her mother urges. "And make an appointment with the eye doctor. I'm off on Tuesday, so I can take you."

"Alright," she says quietly. "I love you."

"I love you too," her mother says, hugging her tightly again.

"Bye bye, Lex. Love you," her father says.

They pull the door shut behind them. It's a decent goodbye, she thinks. She watches them through the sidelight window where her mother has hung one small glass ornament on each pane to catch the sun. Small bursts of color.

Their voices trail off as they walk toward the car, which her father has left running in front of the house. The red SUV pulls out of sight, a puff of exhaust kicking out of the tailpipe. She watches until the small cloud dissipates into nothing.

"Goodbye," she says.

The Call

My hands are shiny with olive oil when my phone rings. In front of me on the kitchen counter, there is a cookie sheet with an array of zucchini, red peppers, and little pieces of broccoli—reds and greens spread on top of glinting silver. I wipe my hands on a towel draped over my shoulder. It's May 23rd, 2016. My parents' 46th wedding anniversary.

Any minute, my wife Lindsay and I are expecting guests to arrive for the premiere of *The Bachelorette* featuring last season's heartbroken runner-up, JoJo. It's laughable that Lindsay and I, two lesbians in our late thirties, are throwing a premiere party for this show. We're definitely not part of the target demographic and yet all day I've been looking forward to a couple of hours of bad television; to laughing at the people on this show who are looking for love.

My body stiffens when I see my father's number on the screen.

"Dani," he says when I answer, "Alexis is dead." His voice sounds as if it has been run through a strainer to remove all the deeper tones. I don't move. I feel Lindsay's eyes on me, looking to decipher meaning from my facial expression as to whether the news is good or bad.

Earlier that day I'd texted Lindsay, telling her that I was worried about my sister. My parents had left their Pennsylvania home on Friday to go to Florida for a few days to celebrate their anniversary, and they hadn't been able to get in touch with her since Saturday morning, which was two days ago.

"Are you okay?" Lindsay had texted back.

"Stressed but trying to worry based on what's actually going on instead of all the potential/imagined things," I'd replied. Imagined things like my sister being dead, a scenario I'd envisioned countless times in my thirty-eight years. If I'd lived closer, I would have gone to check on her, but I was two hours away, in the suburbs of Baltimore.

"She's dead," I repeat to Lindsay the words my father has just said to me. They come out of my body as an exhale. They're full of air, much more than they are of discernible consonants and vowels, but somehow Lindsay understands. I can tell by the way that her brow, which had been lifted and knitted into something of a hopeful question mark, immediately falls.

I'd expected that this particular instance of worry would end like all the others before it: with a call from my mother or father saying that Alexis had been sleeping, had turned the ringer off, had been drunk or high; that she was in the hospital, but she was okay. She was always teetering on the edge of disaster, walking a razor-thin line between life and death, but somehow, she was always okay.

I feel as though I've been turned inside out, as if the parts of myself that I try to keep tucked in and protected are suddenly exposed, the nerves of my body laid bare. Anyone could reach out to touch them and send jolts of raw, pulsing pain through me.

After I hang up the phone, Lindsay wraps me in her arms.

I let her hold me, but it feels like parts of me are leaking out, like I am this gelatinous thing that cannot be contained. Weeping, I break away from her and walk into the other room where I drape my body over a hope chest and pound my fist once very hard on the lid. Our two dogs come to stand beside me, their shoulders lowered and their heads dropped as if to investigate. I peel my body back and call them to me, but Sully stands his ground, suspicious and wary. Maddie comes and pushes her soft head into my hand.

My phone rings again. My mother's voice comes out in whimpers. "Oh Danielle, I can't believe it."

"What happened?"

My mother begins to tell me the story that I will hear countless times in the coming days as people inquire about the circumstances of Alexis's death. Each time the story is told, the person listening will add information about what we now know was our last interaction with her—my Uncle Jim, Alexis's friend Dylan, my mother and father—each will recount the last time they'd spoken to her. They will say things like *"I just talked to her"* and *"She sounded fine."*

I will listen to these conversations with nothing to add since I hadn't spoken to my sister in over a month and only then at the prodding of my mother, who had handed me the phone unbidden, as she was prone to doing.

Yesterday I'd sent Alexis a text to remind her that our parents' 46th wedding anniversary was the following day. Now I think of her phone beeping and ringing next to her dead body.

"Daddy and I pulled up to the house," my mother says. "It had poured on our way home from the airport. The sky had just opened up. Daddy said that he'd go in first, so I waited in the car for a while. When he didn't come back, I went inside and he was on the phone with 911."

I know without asking that my mother waited in the car

because they were afraid of what they would find inside. Over the years, it had become my father's job to check on Alexis when they couldn't reach her by phone. He'd gone to her apartment countless times and banged on her door, screamed her name through a tiny opening restricted by the chain latch. My father had once described to me the way that his knees shook as he climbed the stairs to Alexis's apartment during one of these checks. For fifteen years, they had both lived with the fear of finding her body, but my father tried to spare my mother from this.

My mother's voice cracks and the rest comes out in bursts followed by gasps. "I ran up the steps. The door to her room was opened a crack. She was on the floor in front of the door. She was blocking the door. I could see her hair spread out. She was facedown. I pushed the door so I could reach my arm in and touch her. She was cold."

My mother's voice drops an octave when she relays this last detail. Cold meant her daughter, her firstborn, was dead.

"You're coming up," my mother says, half question, half statement.

"Yeah, I'm coming."

I'd better pack for a long stay, I think when I go upstairs. I feel experienced at this kind of emergency packing. A few years prior, I'd gotten a call that Alexis was in the hospital and I'd packed for that trip, placing a great many items into a suitcase, knowing that I might be there for a while. I'd stayed a week that time. As I begin putting clothes in a pile, my emotion comes in waves that feel like heat rising from the blacktop. I stand in my closet in front of my shelves of clothes, staring and not knowing what to do next, feeling dizzy. *She's dead? She's dead. She's dead? She's dead.*

I hear Lindsay downstairs on the phone, talking in a muffled voice. I know she's calling the people who were supposed to be coming over to our house. What is she telling them?

Don't come. Dani's sister is dead.

Do I need to pack for the funeral or would I be back home before then? What will I wear? Black, of course, black. You always wear black. Will we even have a funeral? *My sister is dead.* How many pairs of underwear do I need? Socks? *My sister is dead.* Pants or a skirt? Will there be a viewing? One outfit or two? *My sister is dead.*

Lindsay finds me standing in our room, staring off in the direction of the window. I feel paralyzed by all the decisions I need to make. She begins gathering clothes and packing a bag for me, and I am so relieved to have this tiny burden taken from me without having to ask.

"What do you want me to do?"

"I don't know," I say. "Are you coming with me?"

"I can, but we need to figure out the dogs."

The dogs. We are still responsible for these two animals, of course. If we bring the dogs, it means packing food and treats and a crate for Sully who is still enough of a puppy that he eats carpets, shoes, anything in his sight. If we don't bring the dogs, we have to find someone to take care of them.

"I'll want you there later in the week. Maybe you should stay here until we figure out when things will be." *Things. The burial, the funeral.*

"Are you okay to drive?" Lindsay asks. The drive from our house to theirs is around two hours in good traffic.

"Yeah, I think so." I sit on the edge of our bed, feeling disconnected from my body, as if someone else is having this conversation, making decisions about these things. "No," I say, changing my mind.

Lindsay calls a friend to come stay the night with the dogs and we decide that she will drive back to our house in the morning and then later in the week, she'll come back for "things."

While we're in the car, I call my parents again. My father answers.

"Did she kill herself?" I blurt out. It hadn't occurred to me to ask the first time I'd talked to either of them; I'd just assumed.

"Yes."

"Okay." I don't ask how she did it. I can tell from the way he sounds that it was probably pills because if there had been a pool of blood from slashed wrists they would have been more hysterical, certainly my mother would have. Those are the only two options for my sister: pills or a razor.

"Was there a note?" I ask.

"Yes," he said.

What did it say? I want to ask, but fear grabs hold of the words before I can get them out and shoves them back down my throat. Fear tells my body that I am not ready to hear the answer. What if it says she hated me? Or that it was my fault? I believe both things to be true, but I can't bear to hear them relayed to me through her suicide note.

"The medical examiner is here now," my father says. "They're taking photos."

My mind flashes to the slurry of crime shows that Lindsay and I watch: *CSI, Criminal Minds.* They are processing the scene, I think, processing the body.

The body. My sister.

Last Day

THE ONLY THING that she doesn't like about the idea of dying is that she has to do it alone, but that's just the way it is. Now that her parents are gone, she feels the familiar braid of loneliness, fear, and relief weave itself tightly around her.

Was she hearing voices on the last day, or had they subsided, giving her a brief respite from their usual chatter? Was she sure about the decision to end her life, or was she still going back and forth?

In the kitchen, she pulls the now-dry dishes from the drying rack and puts them away, then climbs the stairs to her room to go back to bed for a while. She wonders, as she drifts off to sleep, how many times her mother will call to check on her before they return home on Monday. She prays that when her parents are unable to get in touch with her, they will send someone to the house so that they are not the ones who find her body. She would like to spare them this.

When she wakes it is nearly eleven, but her room is still dark. Her parents' flight should have landed in West Palm Beach by now. She thinks of them wheeling their luggage through the airport and smiles as she imagines her father trying to hurry her mother past all the store window displays.

She tosses off the comforter and walks carefully through the mess on the floor over to the window where she pulls back the blinds. The sun causes her to squint. It looks like a beautiful day.

After digging through her drawer, she dresses in her grey Roxy bikini and grabs a towel from the closet. In the kitchen, she pours herself a glass of white wine and goes to sit outside on the back deck. The sun warms her pale skin and she takes a deep breath, enjoying this small pleasure.

When she was a teen, she used to suntan on the picnic table her father built for the back patio. They often had family meals at that table when the weather was nice, as it is today. Her mother would cover dishes with pot lids to keep the flies off of the corn on the cob and burgers. Her mother's face was always dotted with kernels of corn when she finished her cob and the three of them would tease her.

Things were simple back then. Everyone knew their role in the family. She was the older sister who pushed boundaries and created a path for her kid sister to follow. She was also a bookworm and a super smart honor student. Dani was the athlete, excelling at every sport she tried. Dad was the analytical chemist, the hardworking breadwinner, the caretaker of the exterior of the house. When it came time to repair their front walk, he did the work himself—breaking up the old concrete and laying out a new curved path made of brick and mortar. Mom worked as an administrative assistant at Saint Joseph's University and was in charge of everything indoors, making sure the cabinets were stocked and the house was clean. She also tended the garden and potted the plants. Simple.

When her parents downsized to a townhouse a couple of years ago, she'd felt such despair when she learned that they'd left the picnic table behind. Despite her father's devotion to sealing the wood each year, it had nonetheless weathered, its color faded to rusty reddish brown, the surface split with cracks wide and deep. Even still, she thought they would bring it, but when she'd asked, her parents said there was no room. They seemed so disinterested that she felt odd for asking, as though leaving the table behind was the obvious choice; as though the thing had no value at all.

She gets out her phone and snaps a selfie, then sends it to her friend Dylan, along with a text message.

"Hey you! First warm enough for a bathing suit day. Hope I get some tan. Rocky's song just came on radio!"

A pang of regret moves through her. Dylan will miss her. He has been one of her most steady friends and has seen her at some of her worst moments. On their most recent trip to Europe, her voices had gotten so bad that she'd had to come home early. Another failure. She lies back on her towel and takes a deep breath to calm herself and begins to recite one of her favorite lines from a Frost poem: *Then leaf subsides to leaf. So Eden sank to grief...*

Eden Picasso. She thinks wistfully of the name she had chosen if she ever had a daughter. That was back when her life felt like it had potential, when each day felt like something of an adventure, a thing that could bring some surprising joy. When marriage and a family seemed like things that she might one day have.

Not now. Now, the only thing that brought her relief was the idea that she could end this pain. On her worst days, her depression manifested in physical body aches, but today she feels lighter, unburdened by the knowledge that the end is so close.

After sunbathing for a few hours, dozing off and then waking to the feel of the warm sun on her skin, she rolls up her towel and goes inside to look in the fridge. She opens the container of leftover Caesar salad and pops a couple of croutons into her mouth. She heats a few slices of roast beef in the microwave. In the freezer she finds a small Snickers bar underneath a bag of frozen parsley. She laughs, thinking that her mother had probably hidden it from her.

She refills her wine and sighs before turning to the counter where the pad of paper waits for her. She picks up a pen and scribbles on the top square of a small stack of bound sheets.

Does she hesitate before she begins? Does she consider writing a letter? Something long and detailed?

Mom and Dad,
I love you very much.

She stares at the words. They will know why. Her life is not a life anyone would want to lead.

Tell Dani I love her.
Always.

She draws a heart with a comma and then signs her name.

She puts down the pen. Good enough. If they don't understand, nothing she could write will make them understand. But she picks up the pen once more and scribbles the image of a chicken that she has been drawing on letters, envelopes, and notes since she was in college. It's become her signature, and it feels right to have it there.

Upstairs in her room, she changes out of her bathing suit. She puts on her black Calvin Klein bra and red underwear. She pulls her red sweatpants over them. She chooses an Eagles T-shirt followed by a cream-colored long-sleeve sweater.

Does she think about the future of these clothes as she picks them? Does she consider that these articles of clothing will be the ones that a medical examiner will take off of her body and catalog?

It's hard to find space to walk in her messy room. Her mother is always telling her to clean it up, as if the room was the problem. She clears a space on her cluttered bureau and begins lining up the pills she needs. This is where she's made mistakes in the past—by cramming pills furiously into her mouth and swallowing as many as she could at once. This time will not be like that. She will not wake up in some psych ward burning with shame at another failure. This time it's thought out. She's taking extended-release Seroquel—one of the medications prescribed for her bipolar—so that she will not pass out before she can take enough. Ten rows of ten to work through methodically. *Or maybe it's 120 or 127. The autopsy will only list levels in her blood of each drug, not how many pills she took. They will be written in strange fractions that make no sense.*

When she finishes them, she will start on the rows of Xanax, which will begin to affect her almost immediately, but would not be enough on their own. In her previous attempts she didn't understand the precision that overdosing required. Now she knows that if you really want it to work, it must be calculated.

10 down

20 down

30 down

She pours more wine into her glass from a bottle stashed beside her bed. She's always found it remarkable the way that her body wanted to live, even when her mind wanted to die—that in the past her body had always found a way to filter out the toxins that she'd pumped it with.

40 down

50 down

60 down

70 down

She weeps at the thought of her mother and father, but she carries on.

80 down
90 down
100 down
The Xanax are smaller, thankfully, because she needs to work quickly, but can't force too many at one time and risk vomiting. She sweeps five into her hand, tosses them in, and takes a big sip of wine. She repeats this steadily thirteen more times until all of the pills are gone.

By the time she finishes, she already feels the Xanax taking hold, and she steadies herself on the dresser as she makes her way onto the bed. She feels relaxed, calm. So tired. Her eyes close.

Somewhere she hears a noise. What is it? What time is it? Her body rises out of the bed, as if on autopilot, then she feels the phone in her hand.

She tries to say hello, but it comes out garbled.

"Oh, I didn't mean to wake you. Go back to sleep." Her mother. "Make sure you put the phone back on the charger. Love you."

She reaches for the charger to follow her mother's instruction, but she falls to the floor, lands face down in front of her bedroom door. Something heavy falls on top of her, pressing down on her back. Her breaths come slowly and with effort. It doesn't hurt; it's just hard to breathe, especially with the thing on her back that feels so heavy.

Her breaths become more and more shallow.

Time doesn't exist.

A breath.

Just the rug under her face, the heaviness on her back.

A breath.

Her heart keeps pumping blood even as the rest of her body is shutting down. The brain, the liver, all dying, but her heart still pumps—two ounces of blood with each beat; 2,500 gallons in a day.

A breath.

Her heart. The strongest muscle in her body. It keeps going. Her forty-two-year-old body wants to live, but it cannot overcome these odds.

The time between breaths increases.

Tiny breaths.

Until they stop.

The Jacket

I OPEN THE closet and run my fingers down the arm of Alexis's black leather jacket. She wears it most days, but perhaps she thought it was too warm today. We are both off from school, which means that she is hanging out with Coleen and the pack of skaters they've befriended. Sometimes when our parents are at work, Lex brings Terry, Colin, and Lars over to play Nintendo and drink Cokes from the fridge in the garage. When the boys come over, the house is loud and fun and full of energy. Alexis is usually nice enough to let me join them. I pull the jacket off of its hanger and swing it around my scrawny, pre-pubescent shoulders, then thread my arms through the sleeves lined with red satin. On the left forearm my sister has sewn a tarnished silver peace sign; a flying dove forms the interior part. I suspect that Alexis stole this trinket from some dust-covered box in the attic where my parents stow keepsakes from their hippie days.

Alexis likes to sneak up there and go through boxes. She finds things that are retro enough to be cool and she ferrets them away. I'm filled with both envy of and admiration for my sister. Sometimes she wears a black beret and manages to look adorable in it. Once, she convinced me to wear this same beret to a concert and lent me a sleeveless black tank top with a stripe of tie-dye to go with it, but I looked hopelessly ridiculous in her clothes.

Alexis's face is round and lovely. Her eyes, which she insists are green, have always seemed more hazel to me, but they are beautiful nonetheless. She has a habit of closing her eyes and quizzing each new boyfriend about their color as a way to test their love. If they answer incorrectly, she reminds them constantly of their failure. "You didn't even know what color my eyes were," she says, which sends them swirling about trying to figure out a way to make it up to her.

I slide my hands into the pockets of the jacket and touch the contents, though I already know what I will find. The fingers of my left hand seize upon the small, velvety red bag that cinches at the top. Inside there are smooth, glassy stones of royal blue and deep green. I roll them around in my palm before carefully returning them to their small sack. Further down I pull out a pack of nondescript matches—white with a black line of striking surface at the bottom. I flip the cover open and count the remaining sticks, eleven in all.

I imagine Alexis standing in a cloud of smoke up at the trolley stop where she hangs out each morning with her crew of friends. I envision her face lit up by the flash of a match on the dark, wintery mornings.

In the other pocket, I find a pack of Marlboro Reds and a note folded in an intricate, origami-like way. Her name is written on the outside next to a heart. The first time I opened this note, I couldn't figure out how to return it to its original form, but after my initial panic, I discovered that if I let the paper tell me where it wanted to go, it practically folded itself right back up. I have the creases memorized by now. It's a love note from someone named Mike who thinks my sister is beautiful. As my eyes scan the lines, I wonder whether any boy will ever profess his love to me with such wild abandon as Mike does to her. Alexis doesn't like Mike that way. He has a head of curly hair and a bit of acne on his chin and she's told me that she thinks he's kind of nerdy.

In the breast pocket of her jacket there is a single foil-wrapped stick of gum, which Alexis has told me in the strictest confidence is her "hook up" gum. A thrill ran through me when she shared this detail, a feeling that I'd been let into her inner circle. From time to time, Alexis surprises me this way, by telling me one of her secrets, but only after I swear to God I won't tell anyone else. And I don't. I'm hungry for her secrets and I know that one slip on my part will stop their slow drip altogether. Once, she showed me faint red lines on her wrist where she dragged a razor across the delicate skin. She explained that it helped her to have a wound on the outside that matched what she felt on the inside. After that, I cut myself a few times to see what it was like, and I felt a strange relief as I watched the blood seep out. I liked the way it seemed that nothing could stop it once the skin was opened up. And, just like she said, it felt good to have a wound that matched the incredible loneliness that resided inside of me.

I walk outside to our small patio and stand near the brown rainspout where I am shielded from the neighbors' view by a tall hedge. A silver ring taps against one of the jacket's buckles, making a faint tink-tink sound when I walk. Alexis stole the ring from the merry-go-round that our family rides every year in Ocean City, New Jersey. It's one of the few carousels in the country that still has a wooden dispenser arm that gets loaded with rings, which the riders then lean out and grab as they pass by.

Most of the rings are silver, but one is brass, and the person who grabs it gets a free turn on the ride. Whenever we visit the boardwalk in Ocean City, all four of us mount wooden horses on the outermost row and spend an hour or more going round and round, standing in the stirrups and stretching each time we pass the dispenser, hooking our fingers, grabbing a ring, celebrating wildly when one of us gets the brass. Even though I am only twelve, the symbolism of the silver ring adorning the jacket is not lost on me. My sister lives in a space between cynic and dreamer. It represents loss, possibility, and a rejection of conventional values.

I open up the pack of cigarettes, pull one out, and put it between my lips. The match flares to life after one swift pull against the rough black striker. I'm impressed with myself. I lift it up and suck in until the tip of the cigarette glows orange. I practice standing like Alexis—left hand on hip, right foot out in front of the left, cigarette held loosely between the pointer and middle finger. I take a deep drag, turn my face to the sky and exhale. I watch the smoke curl in on itself and slowly disappear, carried away by a light breeze.

The Drive

Is THE RADIO on or off on the drive to Philly from Baltimore? I don't recall, but it feels like it takes forever to get there. I'm conscious of the landscape passing by, but we are not moving quickly enough. I have contradictory impulses warring inside—an urgent need to already be there and a desire to never arrive. The traffic on I-95 is light and I am vaguely conscious of the many familiar exits and landmarks we pass. As we cross the Tydings Bridge, I look in the direction of Father Martin's Ashley, the very first rehab Alexis ever attended sixteen years ago. I drove there every Sunday for the four weeks she was there, full of hope that after she got out, things would be better. Later, there were other rehabs that I never saw the inside of.

"What are you thinking?" Lindsay asks a couple of times as she drives.

"I don't want to see her body," I say once in response, and then later, "I'm afraid of what she might've written in the note."

After what feels like both too short and too long, we are

only a couple of miles away, so I call my parents. "Is she still at the house?"

"No," my father says. "They took her about an hour ago."

She's gone, I think, both relieved and stung at this news. I imagine Alexis's body in the back of a cold, empty vehicle. I wonder if a body can be frightened or lonely. I want to be there with her so that she will not be alone or joked over by some callous funeral worker, but I also do not want to be there.

"Little Jimmy and Stephanie are here. And Aunt Bern," my father says.

I guess that I should've expected this. Years ago, when my grandfather died, my relatives gathered at my parents' house in this same way. They all came over—cousins and aunts and uncles—and spent the day watching home movies that we'd shot over the years and sharing stories about my grandfather—the time he got caught stealing coal from the train car, the time he and my grandma had tried to get married before he shipped off to war.

I was absent from the day's remembrances, but my mother and father and sister told me how nice it had been. Earlier that morning, after spending the weekend helping care for him, I left to return to Baltimore. Lindsay and I were in the early days of our courtship, and I was excited to get home to her. My grandfather had woken up chipper and eaten a big meal for the first time in days. He'd even asked for a cookie. The tiniest part of me thought, *Oh, he's all better now*, but his legs and lungs were full of fluid and his heart was barely pumping. Later, I learned that this type of resurgence was a common occurrence right before someone died—people sitting up one hour and dead the next.

I felt relieved that I missed the moment of his death; the idea of sitting with his body and waiting for someone to come and issue a death certificate frightened me.

I was also oddly glad to miss the day of remembrance with my family. I didn't like long goodbyes. Didn't like things to be dragged out or sadness to be wallowed in. I liked to move along. Keep going. That was the only thing to do in this life, it seemed to me even back then.

I'd been saying goodbye to my sister for years, watching as small pieces of her drifted off, never to be seen again, and yet somehow I'd come to believe that there would always be more: more time, more pieces to lose, more sad goodbyes, so much so that I felt shocked by the news of her death, and then shocked to feel shocked. I'd thought that I'd been braced for impact—hands placed on top of my tucked head, the way they show in the airline safety booklets. This is what hope does to us.

By the time I get off the phone with my father, Lindsay and I have almost made it to the back roads that lead to my parents' house. We're stopped at a red light, the turn signal blinking on, off, on, off.

I feel unreasonably angry that there are other people at the house. I don't want to see anybody except my parents.

"Fucking Jimmy and Stephanie are there," I blurt out angrily, aware that I am out of balance but unable to control it. "Like I really want to see them right now."

Touch of Grey

AT TWELVE, MY favorite nights are when Alexis invites me to sleep in her room, but these invitations don't come without strings attached. Tonight, for example, I had to agree to watch one of her beloved horror movies with her because she is too afraid to watch them on her own. I hate horror movies and though I try to pay very little attention to this one, I have nightmares for weeks afterward and I'm unable to go upstairs or to the basement by myself. A high price to pay, but well worth it in my mind. Sleeping in her room is like having backstage passes to a favorite band. During these times, late at night, Alexis shares her secrets. She thrills me with stories.

Tonight she tells me of her first experience smoking marijuana. She says that pot gives her the sensation that she is floating outside of herself, a different feeling than the one she gets from alcohol. With alcohol, she explains, she always feels she could reign herself in if necessary, "sober herself up" is how she puts it. Marijuana is different, more intense. She likes it.

I lay on the bed, listening and feeling confused. Up until this moment in my life, I have firmly equated drugs with pure evil, the way that they have been portrayed to me in the media—in the commercials they show on T.V. and in Nancy Reagan's "Just Say No" campaign. There is a war going on in America, a war against drugs, and I have been an active little soldier marching dutifully and without thought. During this conversation, however, two things that have always stood in separate spheres collide—the evil of drugs and the goodness of my sister. My brain feels unwillingly stretched. Although I do not know it then, this night marks the beginning of my awareness that things, even drugs, are not purely bad or good.

Curiosity stirs inside of me. *What does it feel like to float outside of yourself?* I wonder, and the instant the thought enters my consciousness, I want it to go away. I want black. I want white. I want things pure and simple and clean. I stare wide-eyed into the darkness and up at the ceiling where my sister has laid out a planetarium of glow-in-the-dark stars. She continues with her descriptions of drugs, and I cannot quell my curiosity as I listen. She tells me her secrets and I simultaneously cringe and embrace the reactions they elicit as everything that I thought I knew begins to feel foreign. I lie there wrapped in mixed emotions, fearful of the thoughts that race through my mind, and the cracks that are beginning to form in the fragile shell of my innocence. Still, I cling to every word. I sense that my sister is trying to give me a gift, a touch of grey to help me think outside of the small box that is my mind.

Give Thanks

"DANI, I HAVE to tell you something," Alexis calls to me through the door of the guest bedroom at our parents' beach house. "I have to tell you something, but you have to promise not to tell Mom."

It's one o'clock in the morning the night after Thanksgiving of 2013, and my sister has just cut her wrist. Not her wrists. Her wrist. Singular. She gave her right wrist the night off. I'm thirty-six years old and she is nearly forty.

I'm asleep in my bed when I hear her voice. I'm groggy and annoyed that she has woken me. I do not yet know that she's raked her wrist with a knife. Lindsay is in bed next to me, our two dogs are curled in tight balls on the floor. We are visiting my family for the holiday. Several hours earlier we were eating turkey and stuffing at the dinner table.

"I'm sound asleep," I say gruffly. "Go to bed."

Earlier in the evening, my sister emerged from her bedroom, freshly showered. She'd put on makeup and gotten dressed for dinner, which was a change from the days on end that she sometimes went without getting out of bed. Her hair was dyed a deep shade of auburn. She'd blown it dry and parted it, rather severely, on one side. She filled her wine glass and moved toward the turkey where she lifted the tin foil to inspect. As she replaced the wrap, a plate of cookies tucked back on the counter caught her attention.

"Oooohh," she said, grabbing a chocolate chip.

"Will you get out of there!" my mother said.

By the time we sat down at the dinner table, my sister was slurring her words, but my family had become accustomed to pretending not to notice her drunkenness, so my father said grace and listed all of the things we had to be thankful for. I was thankful not to be sitting next to Alexis.

I hear my sister walk away from our bedroom door, down the short hallway, and into her room. My parents are asleep in their bedroom, which is on the opposite side of the house. I listen, trying to decipher the noises and translate them into a picture. A shuffling—*now she is getting in bed*, I tell myself, *now she is going to sleep*. I hear muffled voices from the T.V. in her room.

Suddenly, a deep wailing moan rises up. It feels like it goes on forever before it breaks into smaller sputters. I sit up, alert, my spine rigid. The dogs stir. One moves to the edge of the bed and nudges my hand. I stroke her head absently.

"What should I do?" I ask Lindsay.

"I don't know. I think you handled her okay."

"But listen to her."

Alexis is talking to herself, screaming, crying. For the past year I've been going to therapy every few weeks, trying to learn how to have a relationship with my sister that does not consume me. We talk a lot about the importance of boundaries in our sessions. I wonder what my therapist would advise at this moment. It feels like having a relationship with my sister requires that I cut myself in half and allow her to inhabit my interior. As a child and into my teens, I idolized Alexis. I used to tell her that she was the only person in the world who I'd die for without a second thought, and I meant it. I wanted to be like her or to be her, I wasn't sure which.

At the present moment, however, I cannot bring myself to move from where I sit on the edge of the bed, which is strange because if I heard any other human being crying like this, I would go to them and offer comfort, but not my sister. I'm afraid of her, afraid of the ability she has to peel parts of me away, to find the most tender areas and then cast words there that burn like an iron rod just drawn from the fire.

"I call you the Tin Man," she recently said to me, "because you have no heart."

Those words burrowed inside of me and caused me to question my very core. After she'd said that, I kept conjuring images of my parents sitting around with my sister, gossiping about me. "Have you heard from the Tin Man?" my sister would ask in these scenarios, and then everyone would laugh heartily.

When she told me the nickname, I knew she hoped to elicit a reaction. We'd grown up together, confessing our secrets. In many ways, she is still the person who knows me best.

Yet now the name fits. I have closed myself off from my sister. Whenever I am around her I am on guard, trying to keep her from finding a weakness. When we hug hello or goodbye, my body is robotic and tense. When we speak to one another, I share only the most superficial details of my life: funny stories about the dogs, odd tidbits about work. I try not to get stuck alone with Alexis and I am vigilant about how long I stay on the phone with her because I feel the effects of our conversations for days or weeks afterward.

As I sit on the bed, listening to her wail, I know all too well that if I go to her right now, she will reach into my chest and wring my heart out like a dishrag. Even if she doesn't mean to do it, she will. She will circle the past events of our lives, chronicling all the ways that I have wronged her, all the ways our parents have wronged her. I've sat with her before when she was hysterical like this. I've allowed her to take me on a tour of all of her pain. She is a masterful guide, stopping at all of the key moments in her life, explaining how they have affected her. Things that happened almost thirty years ago play in her mind as if they occurred yesterday, like the day our father called her stupid after she let my hamster go and it scurried down the radiator pipe into the crawlspace. She can point to moments like this and trace a line from them to the present. She can recall the details of these instances with startling clarity. She talks about them as if they represent the bulk of her childhood.

I decide to go to my sister, then I decide to stay put. I change my mind a hundred times in the course of a minute— go, stay, go, stay, go—but I do not move. Instead, I sit on the bed listening to her wail. My limbs feel heavy; my body feels rusted in place. *I am the Tin Man*, I think.

A couple of minutes pass and her moans fade, then she is outside our door again.

"Dani," she says, practically shouting. Her voice has changed. It's more businesslike, more certain. "I need your help cleaning this up." I jump off the bed, knowing immediately with the words "clean up" that she's cut herself.

"Jesus Christ," I say, opening the door. Fear streaks through me.

In a recent session, my therapist told me, "Your sister is perpetually suicidal. Even when she is not threatening suicide with some object, she's killing herself with drinking or drugs." It felt as though she'd just solved a riddle I'd been turning over in my head for years. I'd never have thought to put those words together, but they were true. Perpetually suicidal. They were beyond true.

When a person is suicidal there are lists of things to do: you talk to them about it, you call someone, you take their threats seriously, you get them to a medical professional, but when they are suicidal all the time, what is one to do? My family had become immune to the worry that the threat of suicide should cause. We'd lost our ability for vigilance. When everything was an emergency, nothing was an emergency. The possibility of suicide hung over us—an effervescence, never quite materializing, never quite vacating. It was part of the air we breathed and none of us could ever truly relax. This was one of the reasons I felt so angry with my sister.

Alexis begins babbling incessantly as soon as I come out of the bedroom. Her wrist is raw from where she has drawn a knife over it many times, red and raised. There are a couple of places where she has cut through her skin, but she is barely bleeding.

"C'mon," I say as I walk her back to her room. Smears of blood dot the bedspread. A pile of bloody tissues sits next to a plastic bag full of medication. Next to that, she has set a sharp knife with a black handle—one of the serrated ones that my parents use to cut their morning grapefruit.

My mind scrolls through all of Alexis's suicide attempts, measuring this one against the others. This one is no worse than the time she'd tried to get creative, thinking she could put her head in the oven like Sylvia Plath.

"Did she just put it in there and bake it like a hamburger?" she'd asked when she called me.

I'd almost laughed at the absurdity of her question, but I could hear the slur in her words and then she told me that she'd cut her wrist and that it was staring at her, like an eye.

Her past attempts typically resulted in a trip to the psych ward where the doctors—who knew nothing of her medical history aside from what they gleaned from my distraught parents during intake—would change a few medications and then send her on her way a few days later. There was never any sort of long-term plan or care. Occasionally the doctors would recommend outpatient therapy or rehab. She'd gone to both over the years and had gotten better for a time, but eventually circled back to where she was now.

"I tried to cut it this way," she says. "I used this knife. I tried so hard. I tried stabbing." She makes a downward motion with her fist. "I stabbed it. I've always loved the knives here. They're so sharp. I stabbed at it like this. I tried so many times." She curls into a ball on the bed. "I'll figure it out."

I grab the bag of pills and the knife. "Don't take my medication," my sister says as I walk out. "I need that." I ignore her and walk to the kitchen where I drop the knife in a basin of soapy water.

"Did you take any of this?" I ask when I come back.

"No," she says softly. I believe her because the bag is tied at the top and there are no bottles scattered. She is too drunk to do anything neatly.

If you're going to kill yourself, just do it already, I sometimes imagine screaming at her, so loudly that it would cause her hair to blow in the breeze of my angry breath, the way you see on cartoons. Her body would bend backward at ninety degrees and mine would give chase, both of us rubbery versions of ourselves.

It's an awful, horrible thought, but I have a lot of these. I don't verbalize them because I know better than to say most of what runs through my mind. I know that I will regret so many things when she is dead. Things I've said, things I've failed to say, things I've done and failed to do. I want the list to be as short as possible, so I've trained myself to swallow nearly every thought, each of which feels like a handful of jagged rocks sliding down my esophagus, tearing, scraping, until they reach my stomach, where they sit, a ball of churning hardness raking my insides.

I go to the bathroom for supplies, but can't find anything to help clean her wounds. *For Christ's sake,* I think, *how can there be nothing in here?* The house should be fully stocked. Shelves of bandages, gauze, antibiotic ointment. A suicide first aid kit. "I can't find anything to clean the cuts," I tell my sister. "Get in bed or I'm calling 911."

911 as a threat, brilliant, I think. I should call. I know I should call. Any sane person would call. If another human runs a knife over her wrist, it seems obvious that medical attention should be sought, regardless of whether or not the injury is life-threatening, and years ago, this would have been an automatic response, but after seeing Alexis get carted off to the psych unit so many times, the automatic response became a thing that had to be weighed against a set of things that sat on the opposing side of the scale. The most prominent of these was determining which hospital she'd be taken to, because once you called 911, the paramedics would take her to the closest place.

My mother has a list of places that she swears she'll never send Alexis back to. Places that have roaches and mice skittering around. More than anything, our mother seems to dread sending her daughter to a place that is dirty. I suppose she figures that if nothing else, at least she can provide Alexis with a clean bed. A room free of vermin.

Although I have a slightly more objective point of view when it comes to these things, I also have a distorted sense of deference to what my parents determine to be the best course of action when it comes to my sister's suicide attempts. It's a deference born out of overwhelming guilt at the fact that I don't have to deal with my sister's ups and downs on a daily basis. I'm not the one who will sit in a chair next to her bed and see the things they have to see. My parents are her caretakers; they are in the trenches with her, not me. I'm just the relative who swoops in from another state during a crisis, with grand ideas and judgments about how they should handle things. Even when Alexis had her own apartment, my parents were constantly ferrying her to doctor's appointments or to the grocery store or to pick up her medications.

My sister continues babbling, recounting the exact details of how she stabbed her wrist.

"I can't listen to this," I tell her. "Get in bed and I'll rub your head. You need to go to sleep." I begin stroking her head.

"Just breathe," I say. "Deep breaths in and out. In and out." I remember the way she used to read to me, the way I felt so safe when I was nestled into the crook of her arm in her bed.

She breathes deeply through her nose, but between each breath there is more babbling. "You hate me," she says. "I love you even though you hate me."

"I don't hate you. I love you very much," I say, even though the words feel false and hollow. "Just breathe."

"Like I'm meditating?"

"Just like that." She breathes. "That's good," I say. For a moment, I think that this will work. I rub her head and think about the fact that this is probably what she wanted all along—someone to be with her—so she didn't feel so alone.

"I stabbed at it this time," she says. "I thought it would work better if I stabbed at it." Every time she describes what she's done, it feels like she is filleting the flesh right off of my body.

"If you don't stop talking about this, I'm leaving. I can't listen to you talk about how you cut yourself." My tone is one that I would use with a child, trying to lay out clear expectations for her behavior and the consequences that will result if she fails to meet those expectations.

"Don't leave."

"Then stop talking and breathe." She sucks a deep breath in, and then blows out. Her lips form a small "o" when she does this, like some prehistoric fish.

"But I stabbed at it…"

"Do you want me to rub your head?"

"Yes." Pause. "But I stabbed it."

"I'm leaving," I say. I walk out of the room, back to Lindsay who is sitting on the bed waiting. There is more wailing, then a loud bang.

"What was that?" Lindsay asks. I run back to my sister's room. The door is locked, and she is talking to herself, crying and talking to herself.

"I'm calling 911," I say.

Recently, my therapist pointed out that my sister could outlive us all: mother, father, me. A strange noise came out of me in response to this idea—a cross between a snort and a laugh. If I'd been sipping milk, it would've sprayed right out of my nose. Her words struck me as the most absurd thing I'd ever heard, even though a tiny part of me knew it was a remote possibility, akin to hitting the lottery, the kind of thing that you could dream about, but not plan your life around.

"Get your parents," Lindsay says. I don't know why she says this. I expect her to give me rational advice, to tell me to call an ambulance. I wonder whether it's possible that she has been taken in by the strange dynamic that exists in my family. Or perhaps she's simply trying to protect me, to shield me from the anger that my mother and father will have if I call without consulting them.

"No. They're gonna tell me not to call." I punch 911 into the phone, but instead of hitting *send*, I walk toward my parents' room on the opposite side of the house. If my life at this moment were one of those "What's Wrong With This Picture?" games that you see in magazines, there would be red circles all over. I can see this, yet I continue walking toward their bedroom, compelled by guilt over the fact that tomorrow I will pack my bags and return to Baltimore while my parents will be the ones to bring my sister clothes at the hospital—sweatshirts and sweatpants with no strings. They will see the roaches skittering across the linoleum. They will answer the phone when she calls crying because she is scared of the guy who comes to her door at night and touches his penis while he tells her how much he loves her hair.

I stand in the doorway of their bedroom for a moment, listening to their breaths. My father snores.

"Mom and Dad," I say quietly. Nothing.

I raise my voice. "Mom, Dad." Still nothing.

"MOM, DAD."

They both jump. I wonder how many more times they can stand to be startled awake like this. "Alexis cut her wrist. I'm calling 911. She locked her door."

"Wait a minute," my mother says groggily. She walks toward my sister's bedroom and knocks. "Honey? Open this door."

My father trails behind her in his white undershirt and underwear, looking lost, exhausted.

My sister unlocks the door.

"What did you do to yourself, honey?"

"Nothing," she says. "I don't know what you're talking about." My sister has backed into the corner of the room and has put on a long-sleeve T-shirt to cover her wrist. After she is dead, I will find this shirt and I will wear it to bed at night, looking at the bloodstains that never came out.

Alexis has folded the bloodied bedspread on top of itself. She looks like the craziest version of herself that I have ever seen—her eyes large and black. I walk into the room and unfold the comforter, revealing the blood, as if I need to do this to prove I am telling the truth. She looks at me as if I've betrayed her. I turn to my mother. "She needs to go to the hospital. You're telling me that she doesn't belong in a hospital?"

When my sister hears this, she begins screaming. "I'm not going to the hospital! I am *not* going to the hospital!"

"I don't know where they'll take her, probably somewhere awful," my mother says.

"You're a bitch," my sister screams at me. "You're a little bitch."

I walk out of the room into the bathroom where I start opening cabinets again, staring at the contents without seeing what is there. I am filled with anger over the fact that my parents are not going to call an ambulance, and filled with even more anger over the fact that I will not call one either.

"You used to keep my secrets. I used to be able to trust you, but now you're a little bitch," she screams.

A scoff comes out of me as I squat at the bathroom vanity. I want so badly to scream things back at her, to tell her that *she* is the bitch. *She* is the problem, *she* is the one making this family crazy, but I say nothing. I swallow the words and feel them scraping around inside.

My mother coaxes her into bed; tries to calm her down. "It's okay honey," she says. "It's okay."

I go back to my room where Lindsay and I sit facing each other. Blood pumps in my ears. I ball my hands into fists and squeeze while I take deep breaths.

"If it were up to me, I'd put her in a hospital," I say. "I wouldn't give a shit if there were mice or cockroaches. I wouldn't care if a goddamn cockroach crawled on her fucking face." I can feel Lindsay's eyes on me when I say this, but I cannot bring myself to meet her gaze. She rubs my hand, but I wonder whether it is hard to love me in this moment, seeing me so filled with this seething anger.

After a while, the noise in the house dies down. I walk into the hall and see that the light in my sister's room is off. My mother is still inside. I imagine her lying in bed with my sister, cradling her. *How many nights has my mother spent this way?* A jolt of jealousy runs through me.

Sisters in the Night

ALEXIS AND I are in the backyard. It's past midnight and our parents have finally gone to bed. Alexis is home for another weekend visit from college. She hands me the pipe.

"Act like you're taking a drag on a cigarette," she instructs, "but suck in as long as you can and then hold it until you can't anymore, okay?"

"Okay," I say. I'm giddy with anticipation, curiosity.

She lights the pipe and I do my best to follow her instructions. The smoke burns going down my throat and I immediately cough it out.

"Holy shit, that hurt," I say. Alexis laughs.

"Do you want to try again?"

"Yeah."

The lighter sparks into a flame, throwing strange shadows onto my sister's face. I suck on the pipe, watching the flame get drawn down into the bowl where it ignites into a glowing orange ember. I manage to inhale and hold it down for a few seconds before exhaling and coughing all over again.

"Are you okay?" Alexis asks, laughing.

"Uh-huh," I manage in a raspy whisper.

She puts the pipe to her lips and sucks the flame down, taking a long pull and inhaling easily. I feel like a kid watching her fluidity and am suddenly embarrassed at my incompetence. I study her in the dim light, wishing that we looked more alike. Alexis has my father's round face and short stature. Her long brown hair, which she often wears pulled to the side with a small rhinestone clip, is full of golden highlights. Her hazel-green eyes stand out in a face full of otherwise delicate features—a small chin and a smooth, round nose. I have spent hours studying my own face in the mirror, hoping to find some similar traits, but I am my mother's daughter through and through. I've inherited her sharp, pointed nose and her plain blue eyes.

Alexis exhales the smoke into the dark night and I watch her, making mental notes to myself as I've done for years about the way she carries herself, the way she acts. She left her old black leather jacket behind when she went away to college and I still pull it out of the closet from time to time and stand on the patio with a cigarette held loosely between my middle and pointer fingers, trying desperately to imitate the stance I've seen my sister take a thousand times. I never get it right.

We go back inside and turn to the T.V., staring idly.

"How do you feel?" she asks.

"Fine." I shrug. "Normal."

2001: A Space Odyssey is on.

"This is a great movie to watch when you're stoned," Alexis says.

I shrug in vague agreement. I've never seen it before, but so far it seems boring to me. This man keeps talking to his computer and 2001 seems like a really long way off. I'll be an old person by then, twenty-four. I wonder if this is what the future is really going to be like. I hope not; I've always preferred the vision put forth in *The Jetsons*—robot maids and hovering cars. The corners of my mouth lift into a spontaneous smile. I begin to laugh. What was that maid's name, anyway?

"What?" Alexis asks, eyeing me.

"The Jetsons," I say, giggling. "Remember the maid?"

My sister laughs too. We look back at the T.V. and both burst out in hysterical fits. We curl on our sides, holding our stomachs, trying to keep quiet.

And then, as suddenly as it started, the laughter dries up for me. I sit up and go back to the movie.

"What's wrong?" Alexis asks, still laughing.

"Nothing, I'm just...fine."

"Sometimes it doesn't really work the first time," she reminds me.

"Yeah, I know," I say, disappointed.

Thicker Than Water

"GIVE ME YOUR hand," Alexis urges. "It won't hurt. Watch."

She jabs a pin into the cushion of her pointer finger and barely flinches. A tiny dot of red appears. She licks it. "Now you."

My six-year-old self wants to please my sister, but even after this demonstration, I hesitate before pulling my hand from behind my back.

When I finally do, she grabs my finger and pricks me.

"Squeeze some out," she instructs, showing me how to press just below where she jabbed. I follow her lead and watch as a drop of blood materializes on each of our fingertips.

"Okay, are you ready?"

I shake my head solemnly and hold my finger up. She raises hers and slowly we press them together.

"There," she says. "Now we're blood sisters."

Arrival

SHE'S DEAD, I tell myself when Lindsay and I pull into the parking spot across from my parents' townhome. On the drive up here, these words bounced around in my head like a super ball thrown in a brick room. She's dead. She's dead. She's dead. As we passed Aberdeen, drove by the Maryland House, got off of I-95. She's dead.

As Lindsay turns off the car's engine, I recall all the times in my life that I've pulled up right here with a stomach full of dread over seeing my sister, over the uncertainty of which version she would be on the upcoming visit. There were so many: exuberantly happy and talking nonstop; full of anger and sharp words; depressed lump under a tangle of blankets in a darkened bedroom; paranoid foot shuffler mumbling endlessly about people getting into the Wi-Fi and stealing her passwords. The days leading up to my visits were always filled with worry about whether she'd be drinking or high on medication, her pupils wide or small, or whether she'd be closer to the version of the sister I grew up with, the spontaneous and goofy girl who loved mischief.

Now I realize that anxiety is gone forever. This knowledge hollows me out. I yearn for it, for anything other than what I am feeling right now. I take a deep breath. Lindsay squeezes my hand.

My father meets us at the door. Seeing his pained expression cuts through the hazy, dreamlike aura I've been enveloped in since getting the call. It's as if a magician has pulled a blanket off of an enormous ball of sorrow inside of me and set it rolling down a steep hill. It gathers momentum and then there is no stopping it. When my father and I hug, we begin to weep violently, our bodies shaking. We hold each other in a fierce embrace until it feels as if the sorrow has reached the bottom and the frenzied energy comes to a gradual stop.

My father turns to Lindsay. "Thank you for coming," he says as he leans in and hugs her.

"I'm so sorry," she says into his shoulder.

When they separate, I study him. Aside from his red eyes, he doesn't look different. If I met him on the street, I'd never guess that he'd just lost his daughter. His dark, earth-colored shirt is tucked into his pants. He wears Nikes. *Nikes.* I'm not sure what I'd expected, but not sneakers. Not the kind of shoe that you wear to exercise.

"What did the note say?" I ask. I've decided that there's no sense in putting it off.

"It just said that she loved us and to tell you she loved you."

I squint, trying to decide whether or not I believe my father. Would he lie to me if it said something horrible? Would he lie to protect me?

"I want to see it."

"The police took it."

"What? Why?"

"I don't know."

"Where's Mom?" I ask, even though I can hear her voice

coming from the kitchen, where people are speaking in hushed tones. My father motions to the other room.

My cousin Jimmy and his wife Stephanie are sitting on barstools at the kitchen counter. Glasses of soda filled with ice cubes sit in front of each of them. Jimmy's hat is pulled low.

When I find my mother, we bury our heads in each other's shoulders.

"I can't believe it," she says in a soft moan.

We disentangle to look at one another. Tears are pooled in her blue eyes. "I'm moving," she announces, one finger pointed in the air for emphasis. "I can't stay in this house." Her body shakes and her voice breaks.

"Okay," I say softly as I place my hand on her shoulder. "Okay."

The rest of the night is a blur. My father keeps asking people if he can get them anything—*Coke? Diet Coke?*—he keeps telling the story of how he found my sister—*on the floor, face down*—about how her body was blocking the door to her bedroom, how he had to push the door open enough to reach her, how her body had been cold, how they'd had a bad feeling when they pulled up to the house.

Questions float around—how had Alexis seemed before my parents left for their trip; what had she said the last time my mom spoke to her? When I think back on this night, I will see it through a fog of mist, the kind that makes lights look more like stars.

Eventually everybody goes home and Lindsay and I go up to bed.

After I brush my teeth, I stand outside of Alexis's closed bedroom door. I force myself to turn the knob and push the door open. If I don't do this right this minute, I feel certain that the room will be forever endowed with some power over me.

I stand on the threshold and take a deep breath. Alexis's bed is covered with plastic bins and clothes. My eyes circle the room's messy perimeter before settling on the spot where my parents found her body. There is a small discoloration on the cream-colored rug, a light yellow and a bluish green— fluids that had leaked out of her body as she died, or perhaps after. I step into the room, avoiding the spot, as if her body is still on the floor. I take another deep breath. Why wasn't she in the bed? How did she wind up on the floor? Of the many times that I'd imagined my sister's dead body, never once had I imagined it on a floor. This, for some reason, feels like an unbearable indignity.

My eyes return to the stain on the rug. Part of me wants to unsee it; part of me wants to stare at it forever. Part of me wants to touch it, to place my hand on it, on the last remaining physical trace of her; part of me is scared of it, as if a ghost of my sister will rise up from it. I step over it and close the door behind me.

Suicide?

"DON'T YOU THINK she would've written more?" my mother asks in the weeks after Alexis died, referring to the suicide note. "A longer explanation?"

I didn't. My sister's life was her explanation. It had been hard. She'd struggled. Suffered. We all knew it. We'd watched. We'd tried to help. We'd failed. What was left to say?

When my mother brings this up, I tell her I can understand why she'd ask this question since my sister tended toward excess rather than restraint, but I do not think that the fact that she hadn't left a long note means something, and I specifically do not think that it means that she hadn't killed herself intentionally, which is what my mother is getting at when she asks.

My mother has a long history of denying things about Alexis—that she was an alcoholic, that she was a drug addict, and most of all, that these two things contributed to her mental instability. In fairness, I think my mother would say that I obsessed over my sister's addictions and rarely gave enough weight to her mental illness.

At any rate, our family has yet to receive the autopsy results from the medical examiner, so questions loom about the official cause of death and it seems that we've each started to come up with our own version of what happened. My mother is hoping that Alexis died in a way more benign than suicide—an accident perhaps, and she's using the note as a piece of evidence to support her theory.

When I talk to my therapist about the brevity of the note, she tells me that often people don't leave notes at all; that when they do they tend to be very short—requests for forgiveness, professions of love. This makes sense. Isn't that what we all ultimately want, I think, to be both loved and forgiven for who we are? What else is there to ask for?

I feel gratitude for the note's very existence. I don't care that it was written on a small square of paper that sat on top of a block of Post-its.

I try imagining how I might feel if Alexis hadn't left a note. I know it would be an altogether different experience; that I would feel a kind of fury, and this seems strange, to have gratitude and fury on opposite divides of a line. Two emotions practically pressed up against one another, with nothing but a small square of paper determining which of these sweeps me away.

Unknown Things

I DON'T KNOW whether the note was still attached to the pad of paper or pulled off when my parents found it. This is one of the details I forget to ask, and later it feels so inane and unimportant that I can't bring myself to inquire, but I keep wondering about it. Maybe my sister removed the small square and set it in the center of the kitchen counter or maybe she left it on top? Maybe she scrawled it out and then went upstairs to swallow all of the pills, or maybe she swallowed them and then came downstairs to say a formal goodbye? I'll never know. I'll never even get a time of death. The only additional information I will ever receive is that Alexis had been dead for at least a day when my parents found her.

Why any of these details matter—the chronology of her last day, the time of her death—I can't say. None of it will bring her back, but still, they feel important beyond measure and I spend the first weeks after Alexis's death scouring her phone and computer, looking through her text messages, pictures, and e-mails, talking to the last people she talked to. I do all of this in an effort to establish a timeline and a context for her death, but the answers I find do nothing to satisfy me. They are like a heavy rain that pours down on the earth after a long drought. Instead of soaking into the hard, dry dirt, most of the water beads and rolls off, causing floods.

When I speak to the woman at the medical examiner's office she explains to me that they cannot determine a time of death for my sister, as they do on television shows like *CSI*.

For a moment, I think that this woman must be lying, like the fiction is the reality and the reality is the fiction. I want to press her, to scream into the phone like the armchair forensics expert that I am. *What the hell do you mean you don't know, you can't tell me whether she died on Sunday or Monday? What about liver temp? What about rigor?*

Instead, I thank her and hang up the phone. I do not want to be the unhinged, grieving relative. That is not me. I am the calm, steady, and reasonable person, a role I've grown up playing; a foil to my sister's emotional extremes.

Beautiful Ophelia

ALEXIS SPENDS HOURS sitting cross-legged on the floor of her bedroom, leafing through the thick pages of her art magazines. Nearly every page contains an image so lovely she feels compelled to run the point of her Exacto blade around and around its perimeter until it's free. It's detailed, tedious work, but she likes it, likes the feel of the blade forging the path dictated by her hand, the way that each turn and the amount of pressure exerted depends only upon her. Not many things in life bow to her will this way. Not her mother, who comes into her room and tries to coax her to come downstairs to get something to eat or to clean up the mess that she is barely aware that she has made. Not her father, who rails at her to get some sort of job, and not her younger sister, who is tender one conversation and savage the next, tossing words at her like *junkie* and *addict*. They are unyielding, each in their own way. Beyond her control.

Hours slide away while she works, and it's a welcome relief to have time pass unnoticed. One by one she tucks the images she cuts into envelopes or photo albums for future art projects. The envelopes have swelled and multiplied in the last months since she moved back in with her parents. She is thirty-six and single once again, having broken up with Matt, who she met at rehab. Matt, who stole money from her and then swore it wasn't him. Matt, with whom she'd relapsed.

She turns the page, sees an image of Ophelia floating face down, hair like a halo around her head. It startles her, takes her breath away. She is nearly moved to tears as she picks up the blade and traces the outline of the pond, careful to get the exact curve of the lily pads that spill forth from the borders. She feels a special kinship with Ophelia, who first lost Hamlet, and then her father. How can people doubt that Ophelia's death was a suicide?

Around five o'clock she hears her mother come in the door from work. She calls up to her in a singsong voice: *Hello, I'm home.* Her mother's feet on the stairs. Her body in the doorway, hands on hips, eyes scanning the scene—the stacks of magazines, the piles of envelopes, the carpet littered with paper scraps, the dirty dishes piled on the desk.

"Have you been up here all day? This room is an atrocity! And you can't even set the goddamn table for dinner? I work all day and you can't even set the table!" With each sentence her mother's voice rises an octave until she is hollering, her face bright red.

Alexis looks up at her mother for the first time, clenches her jaw involuntarily, registers the tightness in her shoulders from hunching over. How long has she been here? If only she could explain herself, she thinks, but words have been abandoning her for quite some time. So often lately, she stops in the middle of a sentence and realizes she can't recall the word she needs.

Since she was a young girl, she kept journals and wrote poetry. Language was her dearest ally, her defense against the chaotic power of her emotions. She poured herself out onto the page and afterward felt a little relief. From the time that she first learned to read, people called her a bookworm, and she took that name as a badge of honor. She used to curl up on a chair in the morning and stay there through the shifting light of day, not noticing the passage of time.

When she started on her various medications, she found that her brain could no longer follow along when she picked up a book. She'd start a page over and over and over before cursing with exasperation and tossing the book aside.

Her psychiatrist had names for these symptoms when she complained of them: language deficits and brain fog. Common complaints, he'd said, from people who were on the number of medications that she was. He'd pulled his pad from his pocket and scribbled out a prescription for Ritalin. She'd watched his fingers gripping the pen as he signed the bottom.

The first dose burned through the brain haze like a hot sun on a foggy morning. She had a clear mind for the first time in ages. She picked up a book and finished it in a few hours. She wrote a letter, cleaned her room. She felt like her old self.

The Ritalin also stamped out her appetite, helping to bring back the slender figure that the other medications had caused to balloon. People began remarking about how good she looked and how she seemed to have so much energy again.

At first she took the pills exactly as prescribed. But after a couple of weeks, the window of energy and clarity got shorter and shorter and the fog began creeping back. She couldn't stand to have this taken away. She'd already lost so much—her job, most of her friends—she'd be damned if she lost this. She began upping her dose, crushing them up and snorting them, and then crashing when she ran out, sleeping for days and days.

She stares up at her mother's angry face. All around her, half-finished projects lie strewn about. Her shoulder blades jut out sharply from her T-shirt. She is all angles and points. *Junkie thin*, her sister has said.

Ideas dart through her mind and then are gone, like frightened fish. Sometimes she cuts the same thing for hours, going over and over the edges of the same image, trying to get the cut perfect.

She looks away from her mother. "I'll be there in a few minutes," she says flatly, as if she has not heard any of her mother's rant.

Break-In

"ALEXIS IS IN the hospital," my father says when he calls. It's December of 2012, the last year that my sister will live on her own or have any semblance of an independent life. I feel my grip on the phone tighten in reaction to the words my dad has just spoken. I wait to hear the details of another suicide attempt. "There was some kind of break-in at her apartment. She fell down the stairs running away."

"Huh?"

"A break-in," he says again.

"What?"

My father doesn't respond.

"Is she okay?" I ask.

"She's all beat up, but yeah, she's okay. We're going to take her home to stay with us. She says that three people came in through her window and they knocked her to the ground, then started kicking her."

"What do you mean they climbed through the window? Which window? She lives on the third floor."

"The front one," he says. "We asked her the same thing and she got upset with us. She said that we didn't believe her."

"Yeah, but how could anyone climb through her window? They'd need a giant extension ladder."

"I don't know. She says it was two men and a woman with a ponytail. One of the men had a red beard. The police came and looked around the apartment, but they didn't find anything to indicate a break-in. Mom and I are going to clean her place this weekend," he says.

"She lives on such a busy street."

"I know," my father says quietly.

"I'll come up to help you," I say after a long silence. My parents have cleaned her apartment more times than I can count. They will go there on a Saturday and spend the entire day on their hands and knees and they are too old for this, so I want to do whatever I can to spare them, but I also need to see the apartment for myself, to search for clues, to piece together an answer to the questions swirling in my brain.

That weekend, my father and I walk up the long flight of stairs that Alexis tumbled down as she ran in a panic from the intruders. I imagine her fleeing—wide-eyed with terror, half-naked, her feet moving faster than her brain could process. I see her misstep, then hear the noise that her body would have made as it hurled to the bottom, where she sprang to her feet and banged on a neighbor's door for help.

When we open her apartment, an overturned kitchen table greets us. It resembles a dead insect on its back, legs in the air. We turn it over together and then stand in the doorway of her bedroom, silently surveying.

I've seen her apartment in ruins before, but this is different, more violent. A heavy three-panel dressing screen looks as though it's been tossed across the room. The table next to her bed is on its side, the many papers and jars of pens are scattered about.

I survey the two windows that face the street. One is occupied by an air conditioner. In front of the other there's a table upon which a small, artificial Christmas tree stands. I step over the screen and move carefully toward this window, where the intruders supposedly entered. A layer of undisturbed dust covers the sill.

"Look," I say to my father. "There's no way anyone could've come in through this window without knocking all of this over."

He nods as if he's already accepted what I am only beginning to grasp: that there were no intruders. That my sister has either intentionally lied or that she truly believes the story she has told. I'm not sure which is the worse option.

My father and I spend the day cleaning. I play detective with each item I pick up—a half-broken wine glass contains remnants of a white pill dissolved in dried red wine. I examine it to see if there are any numbers or markers that could identify it, but it's too far gone. I turn on Alexis's computer and search through her emails. I don't even know what I'm looking for. I'm desperate to know what happened. But I also don't want to know.

Later, when we return to my parents' house, Alexis is there, watching T.V. A purple bruise has blossomed under one eye.

"Hey," I say as I sit down on the floor near where her head rests on the pillow. I stroke her hair while I talk to her in a soft voice, asking her what happened.

She repeats the story about the intruders, about the way they climbed through the window, only in this version there are four people instead of three.

"Lex," I say as gently as I possibly can, "I know something really bad happened, but it couldn't have happened the way you are saying." I tell her about the undisturbed windowsill, about the Christmas tree, and she looks confused.

"Did you have someone over? Was it someone you know?"

"No! No one."

"Did someone you know hurt you? Are you afraid of them?"

"Maybe they broke in through the door?" she asks.

"Your lock wasn't broken," I say. I study her face as she processes my words, trying to determine whether she's lying. Her mouth opens as if to say something, but no words come out. She looks away, shakes her head, as if she's having an argument with herself.

"I don't, I don't...understand."

I stroke her hair some more and we stare at the television screen where two characters banter back and forth while the audience laughs at all the punch lines.

First Morning

"HOW DID YOU sleep?" This is the question on everyone's lips the morning after we went to bed for the first time knowing that Alexis was dead. Lindsay asks me, I ask my father, my father asks my mother, my mother asks me. Sleep has always come easily to me, even in the worst of times, and last night had been no different, a fact that leaves me feeling like I am failing my sister. Dark crescent moons line my mother's eyes.

My father stands in front of a cabinet, doling out my mother's vitamins as he does every morning. He turns the bottles over one by one. The rattling breaks the silence. Pills of various shapes and sizes accumulate on the counter next to a small glass of orange juice. I open the cupboard and stare at the boxes of cereal.

"Do you want an egg?" my mom asks.

"No thanks."

"Linds, do you want an egg?"

"No, but thank you," Lindsay says.

I wonder how all of this looks through Lindsay's eyes, wonder what she is thinking and feeling. Lindsay never liked

Alexis very much. She never said this out loud, but she never needed to. The only version of Alexis that Lindsay had ever known was the one who complained about her Christmas presents as she was opening them; who got drunk at family dinners and dominated the conversation; who ripped me to shreds with one sentence. Lindsay had never met the warm, giving person who loved me fiercely, who had been kind-hearted enough to let me hang out with her friends when I was a lonely, gawky teen.

"We'll use Riley's," my mother says.

My mom knows Erin Riley from her work at Saint Joseph's University where she's been the secretary for the men's basketball team for close to three decades. Erin's family has a funeral home. She walks over to where my father has placed her pile of vitamins and begins swallowing them between sips of juice.

"Do you take vitamins?" she asks, looking at me. I shake my head. "You should!" she says admonishingly. This is a familiar conversation, a script of sorts, where my mother asks me about some habit she considers healthy—taking vitamins, running, drinking orange juice—and then scolds me gently if I tell her it is absent from my life. I'm aware of how necessary these scripts are, especially now.

She opens up her phone book, the one where she has handwritten the phone numbers and addresses of all the people she and my father know, and slips a pair of reading glasses onto her nose. Her pointer finger slides down the page.

When my parents moved into this townhome a few years ago, I was surprised by how modern it was. The kitchen has flat-panel cabinet doors, with squared-off, brushed nickel pulls—it's a style that I've made only a handful of times over my years as a cabinetmaker, because most customers seek more traditional, Shaker-style doors. The counters are dark granite; the appliances stainless; the stove has six enormous gas burners. The floors are made of cherry rather than the more conventional oak or pine, and the chandelier in the kitchen looks like a spaceship. Nobody can figure out how to change the bulbs in it, no matter how many Google searches we do.

My parents' furniture, which is a mix of antiques, feels out of place in such a modern space. They've jammed an oversized, formal dining room table under the UFO chandelier. In the living room, an elegant console table with intricate brass handles is pushed up against the back of their maroon leather couch that you cannot sit on without feeling like you are going to slide right off. In the corner, the china cabinet stands erect, as if guarding the Lenox china that my mother and father had purchased piecemeal over a period of years, as they could afford it.

Shortly after they'd settled into their new home, my sister had been forced out of her apartment. Her landlord, Wally, who had been kind and good to her for years, finally opted not to renew her lease in the wake of a number of complaints from other residents in the building.

None of us were surprised by this turn of events. The very last time she'd been admitted to the psych ward, I'd looked through her phone, discovering more evidence that her mind was unraveling. There was a slew of text messages she'd written to various people, including Wally, ranting about benign things that she'd interpreted as acts of hostility, like a person on the street outside of her apartment listening to his radio, which she told Wally was done to taunt her. She also described hearing the people who lived next door mocking her through the vents. The texts to Wally were long screeds that mostly went unanswered. She'd also texted one of our cousins and some friends.

She'd never once texted me.

How alone she must have felt.

"Yes," I hear my mother saying into the phone. "This is Clare Ariano. I'm calling because my daughter Alexis…" Her voice wavers, cracks, then recovers.

I begin to cry suddenly and violently. I can feel my body shaking as if it doesn't belong to me, but by the time Lindsay's arms wrap around me, the wave of emotion has nearly subsided. Over the next few days, this is the way that my tears come. They surge out of my body without warning and then disappear.

"My daughter Alexis passed away yesterday and we need to make arrangements. My brother Billy used your services when his son, Michael, died? I'm a friend of Erin's."

When she hangs up the phone, it becomes clear that we have a lot of decisions to make. Where and when to have the mass? Burial or cremation? Do we want a viewing and, if so, would we do it the night before the mass or the day of?

We don't know how to answer any of these questions and yet they loom before us. For all of the worrying that we've done over the years about Alexis dying, we've never really discussed what she'd want done in her absence. Her death has been a taboo topic, which seems ridiculous in hindsight. I rack my brain trying to recall any conversation Alexis and I might've had around this subject.

I know for sure that funerals, and especially viewings, had always terrified her. She loved horror movies and no amount of gore seemed to frighten her, but she would have nightmares for months on end after attending a viewing. I'm fairly certain that Alexis would hate having her body stared at and cried over, but what she would or wouldn't want feels secondary to my parents' desires. Although everything in me wants to honor Alexis's wishes, I know that if my parents need a viewing in order to feel closure, I'll keep my mouth shut and deal with it. Alexis is dead; my parents are alive.

Still, I keep scrolling through my brain to recall conversations

Alexis and I might have had about death and dying. I feel an intense pressure to at least try to get every decision right, to do it the way she'd want it done. My inability to answer the simplest questions is a harsh reminder of our estranged relationship.

"She wouldn't want to be buried," I say a bit too loudly, without prompting. It's the one fact that I know for sure.

Her Gift to Me

ALEXIS PULLS THE covers up and tucks me in. "Just one chapter," she says sternly, and I nod obediently. My seven-year-old body quivers with excitement. The walls of Alexis's bedroom are covered with posters she's carefully pulled from the folds of *Teen Beat* magazines. Matt Dillon, Emilio Estevez, and C. Thomas Howell all stare out with expressions that range from boyish to brooding. When I'm snuggled in her bed she feels less like my older sister and more like a friend. I know she loves reading to me as much as I love listening. Alexis climbs into bed next to me and cracks open *The Princess Bride*, which is a very thick—and therefore grown-up—book.

Last night we left off with Buttercup having just pushed the man in black down into the ravine. As the man tumbled down he cried out, "As you wish," which is what Buttercup's one true love, Westley, used to say to her. Up until this point in the story we thought that Westley had been killed by the Dread Pirate Roberts, but when the man in black cried out this phrase, both Buttercup and I realized that the man she'd just pushed off the edge was Westley!

That was the exact moment that my sister snapped the book shut and turned off the light. I'd looked at her pleadingly.

"Tomorrow," she said with authority. "*Unless* you are mean to me." Then she'd curled up next to me and closed her eyes.

This same scene repeated nearly every night whenever Alexis was gracious enough to invite me into her room to read to me. She knew that it was important to leave me wanting more. Our deal was that I had to be nice to her all day if I wanted her to read to me at night. Being "nice" involved getting her iced tea whenever she asked, scratching her back on demand, and giving her the first pick of desserts after dinner. It also meant keeping my mouth shut anytime she did something that my parents wouldn't approve of. This last condition was the easiest part of the deal for me to keep.

The only times I slipped up were when she hit me or put me in a headlock or pinched me with her toes, the latter of which she absolutely loved to do and was freakishly skilled at. Any of these things automatically sent me screaming for my mother, who would then scold Alexis and remind her that she was older and stronger and should know better.

I loved hearing the phrase "You should know better" coming from my mother's mouth. As the younger sister, I was free of the burden of knowing better. While my mother scolded Alexis, I'd wrap my arm around one of mom's thin legs and peek out from behind, my face shiny with tears, and I'd stick out my tongue. Of course, Alexis would get her revenge later when I showed up at her door for our nightly story time, and she would send me off to my own room with the admonishment, "Maybe tomorrow. *If* you're nice."

Today I managed to be nice enough and am reaping the reward. I've spent the day worrying about whether Westley would be okay after his fall down the ravine. Not to mention the looming threat of Prince Humperdinck, who has forced

Buttercup to promise him her hand in marriage under threat of death.

Alexis's voice goes high when she does Buttercup, gets squeaky when she does the Sicilian, and when she does Fezzik, her words roll out slowly in a deep, thick-tongued timbre.

I've been paying close attention to our progress in *The Princess Bride*—how many pages we have already read and how many are left. Part of me wants the book to go on forever so that I can have this excuse to be here snuggled next to Alexis, listening as her voice rises and falls, and the other part wants to get to the end, to know how things turn out; whether they all live happily ever after or whether that's only in childish fairytales.

The thing I love most of all is that whenever there is a word I don't understand, I stop Alexis and she explains what it means. Each time I learn a new word, I feel the world opening up to me and I wonder how I ever got along without that word. I'm hungry for language, for the power to name and express things, and my sister nourishes me. Words are the things that will guide me through my most difficult times; the things that will allow me to process my emotion, and it is Alexis who gives me this gift.

Voices

After the "break-in," Alexis stays with our parents while she recovers. Weeks slide by and soon it has been a month. She's terrified to return to her apartment, but living with my parents is not sustainable. The more time that passes, the more the three of them clash and argue. When she finally goes back to her place, my parents breathe a sigh of relief, but it's not long before she begins calling home to complain about her neighbors.

"They yell at me through the walls," she tells my mom. "They say my T.V. is too loud."

When my mother relays these stories to me, I wonder who the hell these people think they are. I find myself googling the address of the neighbors, which leads me to a property record with the name of the person who owns the rowhouse next to hers. I type the neighbor's name into the search engine and wind up staring at a picture of a lovely blonde-haired woman on the website of a Philadelphia law firm where she is an attorney. I look at the photo, feeling disappointed, realizing that I was hoping to find some proof that this woman was bad news—a mug shot would've been the jackpot, but I would have settled for something smaller, like a quote in a news story that showed she was mean-spirited. But there's just this lawyer picture of her, looking all put together.

I share the results of my online sleuthing with my parents and we try our best to make sense of it. Every time I talk to my mom or dad, this topic dominates our conversations. We volley questions back and forth and put together all sorts of extremely unlikely scenarios that could explain the things my sister keeps describing.

Why would anyone do this?

Do you think it's because she's up all night?

Maybe she makes a lot of noise? Plays her T.V. too loud?

Maybe she has people over to her place and they're up partying?

Do you think she should call her landlord?

"There are some sick people in the world," my mom says. "I mean, really sick. Who knows what's going on!"

Over the next couple of weeks, Alexis continues to call my parents with more and more stories about harassment. All the stories have a similar frame, with the people yelling through the walls for no reason, but then one day the story changes.

"Your sister said there was a man on the roof messing with her cable dish and that he was talking to her through the T.V. Could that happen?" my mom asks me. "Could a technician do that?"

"No Mom," I say softly, realizing that the things Alexis has been describing are not real. I've had countless moments like this before, where the truth has come into sharp focus, only to blur again. This moment is significant not because it's the first time I've had this realization, but because it's the last time I'll need to have it. The time that the haze of denial fully lifts. I feel the familiar tug of both shock and recognition. "Of course" wrapped deeply inside of "I can't believe this."

But my mother can't fathom that some of Alexis's claims don't have a basis in reality, so she makes plans to spend the night at my sister's apartment.

"I want to hear these friggin' people for myself," she tells me the next time we talk.

"What? Where are you going to sleep?"

"On the couch."

"That tiny thing?"

"It's only one night."

I think of my mother with her bad back curled up on the loveseat, listening for things that she'll never hear.

"And what if you don't hear anyone? Then what? Are you going to stay a second night?"

"Well...we'll see."

But before the sleepover happens Alexis calls my mother at work, screaming that she's been robbed. She's hysterical, says her wallet is missing. My mother calls my father. They both leave work and drive down to Alexis's apartment. When they get there, Alexis is limping around, her feet covered with blisters from a pair of shoes that she wore out to a bar the night before. Her T.V. has been knocked off the stand near the kitchen window.

"I was dusting the window for prints and it fell," she tells them when they ask why it's on the floor.

They find the wallet beneath one of the many piles on the floor of her messy apartment. But Alexis insists that someone had been there and robbed her. She points to a brown smear on the floor.

"See that?" she says. "They tracked dog shit in here."

My father gets down on his hands and knees to look at the mark, to smell it, discovers that it's a brownie.

"My feet hurt so bad. They're so sore," she complains.

"C'mon," my mother says, coaxing her. "Let's just go get those feet taken care of. We really should have someone look at them."

"Just my feet?"

"Yes, just your feet. They look so sore."

They go back and forth like this before Alexis agrees reluctantly.

Once they get to the hospital, the doctors call for a psych evaluation and determine that she needs treatment. When Alexis realizes that she's being admitted against her will, she begins shouting. A couple of orderlies take her out of the room screaming.

"Thank God," I say when my dad calls to tell me what happened. "At least we know she's safe now."

"She's pretty angry with us," he says. "She's calling Mom and haranguing her. Saying that if Grandpop knew that we'd put her in a mental hospital against her will, he would roll over in his grave."

I feel the old burn of anger well up inside of me when I hear this. How can she be both so sick and so manipulative? How is it that she can be totally out of touch with reality and yet still know exactly what buttons to push in order to make our mother feel like shit? Bringing up Mom's dead father is a new low.

Alexis gets released a few days later, when her hallucinations subside. In the next months, we find out that her landlord will not renew her lease, so we pack up her belongings and she moves in with my parents. The whole episode is like a deep wound. Every time it starts to heal, we move in some way that opens it up all over again. Alexis refers to it as "the time you had me put away." Years later, when I think of my mother offering to sleep on the tiny loveseat and my father bending down to inspect a brown spot on the floor, I understand deep in my bones that this is what hope looks like.

In Her Apartment

THE WEEKEND AFTER we have Alexis 302ed to the psych ward—the code for having someone involuntarily committed when they are a threat to themselves or others—my father and I trudge up the steps to Alexis's apartment. Alexis has been 302ed several times in the past when she was suicidal, but this time is different and it feels more frightening.

We're here to clean the apartment, which is the last thread of normalcy in my sister's life. Technically speaking, she still lives on her own, even though my mother has to ferry her to doctor's appointments, to the grocery store, to pick up her numerous prescriptions; even though my sister frequently retreats to our parents' home for two weeks or more.

My father and I stand shoulder to shoulder in the kitchen, looking out over the mess in the bedroom area. He lets out a noise, a cross between a sigh and a laugh.

"Holy shit," I say as I take in the chaos. It looks as if a giant of the fe-fi-fo-fum variety has scooped up the apartment in a set of massive hands and shaken it violently. A single path of carpet, which leads from the kitchen to the bed, is visible.

The remainder of the floor is covered. I picture my sister shuffling along this trail.

Shoes sit on top of papers. A bra rests on a dirty plate. An open pill bottle lies on its side, the contents scattered. Piles of books that were probably stacked high have fallen every which way; books about art, books of quotes, books by Nietzsche and Freud and Hemingway and Anne Rice, whom Alexis absolutely loves.

My father walks out into the mess, shoulders slumped, trash bag in hand. He slips on some papers and nearly falls. His arms flail, and as he tries to remain upright, he bumps into a table and sends a glass filled with pens, pencils, scissors, and nail files flying.

"Jesus Christ," he says. We laugh because neither of us thought the mess could have gotten any worse. My father detests clutter. Years ago, before we left the house to go on our annual vacation, he threw away an envelope filled with cash because it was sitting on the counter and he'd been struck by the need to tidy up before we went. Standing in the middle of this mess, he looks both defeated and determined. Today, he gets to have his way with the clutter, to throw things away without protestations rising up from my sister or my mother. He begins stuffing things into the bag.

I bend over and start re-stacking Alexis's books, her most steady and constant companions. As a child she read incessantly—first the *Sweet Valley High* series and then Christopher Pike thrillers that she'd pass onto me, and then it was everything and anything by Stephen King, even though his novel, *It*, terrified her. Finally, she'd graduated to the classics, stealing paperbacks from my parents' bookcase and adding them to her own—classics like *The Gulag Archipelago*, *Catch 22*, *1984*. She and my father would talk about the books when she finished them, a ritual that sparked my jealousy.

Colored tabs of paper poke out from the pages, indicating passages that she must have liked or wanted to remember.

My father grunts with exertion as he shakes out a second black trash bag. How different this exercise of cleaning would be if my mother were here. She would be so much more thoughtful about my sister's things, aware of the fact that the objects in this apartment are the sum total of my sister's thirty-nine years on this earth. I do my best not to think about this aspect of our project, but the truth of it is all around me. The trundle bed she sleeps on is the one she got when she was a teenager. Its chipped white paint reveals a dull, grey metal underneath. The stereo in the corner is the same one from her college dorm.

For my father, the job is simply to create order. If it looks like junk, it will go in the trash. I appreciate the clarity of his way of thinking, but I cannot fully subscribe to it. Throughout the day, I swing back and forth between my father's and my mother's philosophies. I throw stacks of art magazines and envelopes filled with bills from five years ago in the trash, then, consumed by guilt, I stack some of these same things into neat, albeit precarious, piles.

I think of my sister here alone, day and night. Sitting on the floor, shuffling through the mess, talking to herself. One of her great passions is making art out of wooden boxes and picture frames. She paints their surfaces, then collages them with magazine cutouts and literary quotes that she pens with fancy markers. When she finishes projects, they are quite beautiful, but more often than not the images remain in their neatly labeled envelopes: clocks, animals, hands, flowers, etc. I find twenty or thirty of these envelopes filled with cutouts no bigger than a dime. The floor is littered with small scraps. Every time I pick something up, tiny pieces from magazines flutter out and float to the floor.

After a couple of hours, the carpet becomes visible in small patches that I vacuum to give myself a sense of accomplishment.

I need to see progress being made. It's one of the reasons I'm a cabinetmaker. I love seeing things transform. Turning a stack of wood into a nightstand or a bed frame soothes something inside of me. For a short stint after college, I tried teaching in an inner-city school, but I only lasted a year because there was no instant gratification. During cafeteria duty, I would look out at the sea of faces and feel completely hopeless that I could change anything in the lives of those kids.

The air conditioner hums but does little to cool the apartment against early July's stultifying heat. Sweat beads on my father's head, then runs down his face. I can hear his labored breathing as he moves things around. Every so often, I hear him *goddamn* something under his breath.

When we finally uncover the loveseat, we take a break, sipping on sodas that we brought with us. My father wipes his face with a paper towel and lets out a long sigh.

"This is unbelievable," he says. I nod. Everything about my sister is unbelievable to him, as if he lacks the ability to look back over her life and see the trail of dots that constellate so clearly into where we are now. First it was unbelievable that she had to go away to rehab, then it was unbelievable that she relapsed, then he couldn't believe that she'd racked up $60,000 in credit card debt while holed up in a hotel room on a drug binge with her then-boyfriend. Each year a new series of unbelievable things happened, each more unbelievable than the next. The current unbelievable is that Alexis is in a mental hospital because she's been hearing voices.

I look over at him as he tilts his head back to drink from his can of Coke. The sun pours through the window and I see how thin his grey hair has gotten. My mother is always begging him to let it grow a bit longer, but he refuses because he claims it gets too curly.

When we have done all we can do, we carry the trash bags one at a time down three flights to the curb. I try to work quickly so that my father does not have to make so many trips up and down the steps. All this physical labor evokes memories that speed through my mind like a flipbook: my father lugging heavy televisions sets and small refrigerators into our college dorm rooms; my father carrying one end of a couch into Alexis's first apartment; my father standing with his hands on his hips, admiring my first house, sweat on his brow from carrying the dresser into the bedroom. In the earliest memories, he is fit and sturdy-looking with dark, almost black hair and calves that bulge when he bounds up the steps. Now it is I who am sturdy and fit, with a body made strong by breaking down sheets of plywood into parts for cabinets.

Returning downstairs with our final load, we see that a man and woman have begun going through the bags of trash that we've put out. The man wears a baseball cap and a tank top, revealing thin, wiry arms. The woman has a tangle of brown hair pulled on top of her head. Her eyes are sunk into her face. We wait for them to leave before we drop two more sacks on the curb, get in the car, and drive away.

I try not to think about the things that I placed in the garbage bags or what they might have meant to my sister. I tell myself that we had a job to do and we did it; we had to restore some order, for her sake.

And though this is true, what we just did in her apartment was as much for us as it was for her. For the hours that we were there, we were in control—able to make decisions about each item we touched: yes/no, good/bad, keep/pitch. Nothing else in our life with Alexis is that simple.

Planning a Funeral

"I THINK WE should have the mass at St. Phil's," my mother says, "because that's where you both went to school and received all of your sacraments."

My father and I both nod in agreement. "What day should we have it?" my father asks. "It's Memorial Day on Monday." He half mumbles this last part out of the side of his mouth, as if he's unsure he should mention it.

"Yeah," my mom says, as if she hadn't quite considered this. People from the suburbs of Philly typically head en masse to the Jersey Shore for a long weekend. I'm not sure if my dad has brought this up because we don't want to inconvenience anyone who might have plans to go to the beach, or whether we are worried that the turnout at the funeral will be low, or if it has to do with concern over the funeral procession hitting traffic as we drive from the mass to the burial, but it's clear that this is a thing to be considered.

"Do you think we could do it Friday? Or should we wait until after the weekend? Next Tuesday?"

"A whole week? That feels too long," I say.

My mom nods in agreement. "Well, I'll call Riley's and tell them Friday." She picks up the phone and dials. My father pours a cup of coffee. His spoon clinks as he stirs cream into it. Lindsay sits on my parents' slippery leather couch. It occurs to me that I need to call my work, but the thought of saying out loud what has happened feels impossible.

"Linds," I say quietly. "Can you text Ralph and Austin and let them know that I won't be in?"

"Sure, where's your phone?"

"On the counter over there. But can you use your phone? I don't want those texts in there. I don't want to see them next time I use it."

"Okay. What do you want me to say?"

I know she's asking whether or not it's okay for her to say that Alexis ended her life. It hadn't occurred to me that I could choose to keep this to myself. "You can tell them everything. And tell them I don't know when I'll be back to work, but I'll let them know as soon as I can."

Lindsay nods, squeezes my hand, then goes off to look for her phone.

My mother hangs up her phone just then. "The director says she'll call over to St. Phil's to find out if the church is available for Friday." She removes her glasses from the end of her nose.

"Do we have any more milk?" my dad asks.

"In the basement," my mom says. "I'll get it." Her slippers on the wooden stairs make a soft sound that fades as she nears the bottom. My parents have a second refrigerator in their laundry room, which my mother keeps stocked with extra juice or milk.

When my parents moved into this townhouse a couple of years back, I'd stood in front of their new, two-door wonder of a refrigerator, which was a huge upgrade from the rinky-dink model they'd left behind in their old home. "Mom," I'd said as the cold air whooshed out at me, "look how much room you have! And there's a second one downstairs?"

Over the course of my parents' long marriage, they'd evolved when it came to the division of labor, but the refrigerator had remained my mother's domain, and she was famous for stuffing it to the gills. There was a running joke in our family about the inherent danger in opening the freezer, where heavy things were always precariously balanced and ready to tumble out onto one's foot.

The phone rings and I hear my mother's voice in the basement. My father and I rush to the top of the stairs to listen. The half-gallon of milk that she went down to retrieve rests on the bottom stair.

"Oh, really? Okay. Uh-huh. Okay. I'll call you back. Thank you."

"What's the matter?" I ask.

"The undertaker at Riley's said St. Phil's is only available for an hour on Friday."

"Well, that's not long enough. Let's call St. Annie's then," my dad says.

"Yeah," my mother says. "I just think I'd like it at St. Phil's." She looks up at me.

"Yeah, it'd be nice," I say, "but if it's not available...I mean, we don't want to rush through the service." I sit on the top stair. My father stands next to me, leaning against the doorjamb.

"But I think Alexis would want it at St. Phil's," my mom says. This silences both my father and me for a moment. I hear Lindsay's footsteps as she walks up behind me and I feel suddenly self-conscious of how the three of us must look and sound, calling to one another from opposite ends of the staircase, unable to come to a decision on the location.

"Well, we can't have it at St. Phil's. Call St. Annie's," my father says definitively.

"What about St. Dot's?" my mother offers. My mind flashes

to St. Dot's, where I used to go to dances in grade school. In the seventh grade, when I began to finally outgrow my extreme tomboyishness, Alexis would curl my bangs with her hot iron and spritz them with hairspray until they stood up on their own in a small puff. The first time I wore my hair like this, I felt like the nerdy girl in the movies who got a makeover and suddenly had boys at school notice her.

"Why would we have it at St. Dot's?" my father asks.

"I don't know," my mom says. "It's just that she didn't have a connection to St. Annie's." The three of us go back and forth over location until we reluctantly decide that we'll just have to settle for St. Annie's.

"Well, you'd better call St. Phil's and tell them we don't need the church for an hour on Friday," my father says.

Part of me wants to ask my father why he doesn't call St. Phil's, instead of telling my mom to do it, but I know that this is the way that things work in their relationship. My father offers critiques, but rarely solutions. He complains about things that he has no intention of changing, but my mother works through details and gets things done. I see more of my father in myself in this regard—I tend to identify problems and then wallow in self-pity as if I am a victim of them, rather than a person capable of coming up with a solution for them.

My mother nods, picks up the phone, and dials. I get up from the stairs and begin to collect the breakfast dishes and start washing them. Lindsay grabs a towel. It's soothing to have something to do.

As I work, my mind wanders back to the last time I was here doing dishes, just as I am now, only then Alexis milled around the kitchen, mumbling to herself. She came over to me with a stack of mail.

"Can you help me sort through these bills?" she asked.

"Sure, I can help you a little bit later," I said.

"Thank you. I just don't understand these bills. I call

them and ask questions and they tell me things that don't make any sense. I got two bills for the same thing and the girl at the store said that it'd be free, but then I get these bills..." Her voice trailed off.

When she mumbled, it was difficult to discern whether or not she was talking to me or to herself. Her voice would get suddenly louder on certain words. The fourth, tenth, sixteenth. Then I'd hear her tone change to a question, and I'd have to glance her way to see if she was waiting for an answer, but mostly she answered herself. I'd only been home an hour and her near-constant talking already had me on edge. I took a deep breath and reminded myself that I only had to deal with her for twenty-four hours.

"We'll get it figured out, Lex," I said, interrupting her mumbles. She looked up, as if startled to see me, and then nodded before she began looking through her wallet for a card that was missing. She laid all of her cards out on the counter and stared at them in a perplexed way. I looked over at my father to gauge his reaction, but he was focused on reading emails.

At least I was kind to her on that visit, I think now, even if she was driving me crazy. My mom emerges from the basement waving the phone in the air. "You won't believe this," she says as she places the milk on the counter. "Father Steve from St. Phil's says we can have the church."

"What? I thought they were booked," my dad says.

"When I called him to tell him we were going to use St. Annie's, he claimed that he'd told Riley's that we could work something out. I hung up with him and called Riley's and they told me that Father Steve does this all the time."

"Does what?" I ask.

"Riley's said he has some kind of ax to grind with them. That if the family calls, he's as sweet as could be, but if they call, he makes life difficult for them."

"Unbelievable," my father says. "So it's booked?"

"It's booked."

What an asshole, I think about Father Steve as I grab the milk from the counter and jam it into the fridge.

Contagion

LINDSAY, ALEXIS, AND I are squeezed into the backseat of my father's Ford Escape. My mother sits in the passenger seat next to my dad, reading the newspaper, her glasses halfway down her nose. It's the Friday after Thanksgiving of 2015—the last Thanksgiving Alexis will be alive—and we are on our way to the Brandywine Museum. Alexis sits next to me, staring out the window. She has been neither overly talkative nor withdrawn today. She seems normal in a way that I haven't seen her in years. "Oooh, I love this song," she says when my father puts on *Hey Jude*, but she doesn't make any demands to turn it up or to play it again when it ends, she just sings along quietly.

Lindsay and I drove up early this morning from our home in Maryland. We usually spend Thanksgiving with my family, but since Alexis's last suicide attempt two Thanksgivings ago, I've been working to "establish healthy boundaries," in the words of my therapist. I told my sister and my parents that I would no longer attend any gatherings where they were serving alcohol because I couldn't be around Alexis when she was drinking. Much to my surprise, this turned out to mean that I would no longer be attending *any* gatherings. Not Mother's Day brunch or Easter dinner or birthday dinners because my parents could not fathom the idea of hosting a social gathering where alcohol was absent.

Still, every time a holiday rolls around, my mother casually asks me if I'll be coming up to visit, which is precisely what happened a couple of weeks ago.

"Are you coming up for Thanksgiving?" my mom asked.

"Well, that depends on whether or not you're having alcohol at Thanksgiving." We both knew that if there was alcohol, my sister would be drinking.

"Oh," she said, in an "oh this again" tone.

"Mom, c'mon, we've talked about this."

"I know, it's just that Daddy really likes to have his wine."

So do you, I thought, but held my tongue.

"Mom," I said, tears welling up, "I gotta go."

Later, I vented to Lindsay about the conversation. "It's like they don't give a shit whether they see me or not, like it's more important for them to have alcohol than it is to have me."

"It's hard not to see it that way," Lindsay said.

"It sucks. I want to see my family. I *miss* my mom and dad."

"We'll figure something out," she assured me.

What we'd figured out was that we'd come up early on Friday morning, spend the night, and then leave Saturday after my Aunt Nancy and Uncle Gene hosted their annual post-Thanksgiving get-together for the Ariano side of the family. I was gambling on the fact that my sister probably wouldn't go to Nancy and Gene's, but I decided that regardless, I wasn't going to miss this event. If Alexis was there, I would simply do my best to steer clear of her.

Lindsay was less than thrilled about the prospect of a late-night drive home after Nancy and Gene's. "Are you sure you don't want to stay over Saturday night and leave early Sunday?" she asked.

"No, because if Alexis goes to Nancy and Gene's, she'll probably be drinking, and I don't want to get stuck back at my parents' house with her. That gives me major anxiety," I say, shuddering at the thought of another night like the infamous Thanksgiving.

"Oh, I hadn't thought about that," she said tenderly. "Okay, we'll leave from Nancy's then."

Out the window of my father's car, I stare at the leafless trees and then glance over at Lindsay. My father is driving so slowly that behind us on the winding road, a line of cars has begun to stack up.

"Dad," I say a bit too sharply, "you're driving so slow!" When I hear myself, I cringe. A familiar push/pull of emotions rocks inside of me: I want to spend time with my family, but I don't like who I become when I am around them. On a normal day, I'm not the most patient person, but this feeling amplifies tenfold around my sister. Five minutes with her and it feels like all of the patience has been wrung out of me. I am brittle and ready to snap.

When we get to a section of road that opens up to two lanes, the cars behind us roar into the left lane to pass us. I look over at Lindsay and widen my eyes. I crack open a can of Diet Coke that I brought for the ride.

My sister turns. "Oh, can I have a sip?"

I hesitate, then hand the can over to her, hoping to God that she didn't notice my hesitation. The last thing I want is to hurt her, but for as long as I can recall, I've been afraid in the most irrational way that I will get sick the way that she is sick; that I will catch her illness. Not in quite the way that you would catch the flu from someone, but more in the way that if you spend a lot of time around a friend, you might start using phrases that they use. For the life of me, I cannot understand why I am so healthy and she is so ill. We have the same blood running through us, the same family history of addiction and mental illness. We grew inside the same womb, so why am I okay? As children we pricked our fingers and touched them together just to solidify our blood bond.

I'm racked with guilt by this disparity, but I have no noble desire to trade places with her. On the contrary, I have a number of things that I do to ward off the illnesses that I worry might already be floating around in my blood. Not sensible, self-care kinds of things, but things in the realm of doing a rain dance to ward off a storm: I refuse to sleep in a bed that she has slept in, I will not allow myself to empathize with her too much because I fear that my brain might slowly shift to thinking the same way that she does, and I most definitely do not drink or eat from anything after her.

I know these superstitious precautions are ridiculous, but this does nothing to quell my impulse to act on them. Anxiety cannot be quieted by reason. When she hands the can of soda back to me, I know I will not drink after her. *Drink it*, I tell myself, *just take a sip*. But I can't bring myself to do it and I hate myself for it.

Behind us, more cars are piling. "DAD! Will you speed up?" I practically scream.

Secrets

"YOU KNOW," ALEXIS says in a serious tone, "you're not a baby anymore." I study her face, uncertain as to where she's going with this. I'm six years old and she has brought me outside to our backyard swing set to have a talk. My hands are sweaty from where they grip the metal chains of the swing. We sway half-heartedly. I kick a woodchip and send it flying into the thick green grass that our father obsessively trims and keeps free of weeds. "Part of being grown up means that you can't go running to Mom and Dad to tattle about every little thing," she explains. Her voice is quiet and serious, as if she is sharing a secret with me. I've heard her use this tone before, but only when speaking to friends.

"Like last week," she says, "when I broke the fan and you went right to Mom to tell her about it, you can't do that anymore."

I'm suspicious that she's trying to trick me, like the time she slathered my water gun with crazy glue before handing it to me, but I want to believe that she's finally seeing me as a friend rather than an annoying little sister who follows her around every day.

"If you want me to trust you, you have to keep some things secret. Just between me and you." She begins pumping her legs to start swinging, and I follow suit. "Do you understand?"

"Yes."

"Do you promise?"

Her eyes are beautiful and soft. They seem to know a little of everything.

"I promise."

She looks back at me as she reaches the top of her arc and smiles. I pump my legs harder, desperate to keep up.

First Attempt

I HAVE MY face pressed close to the bathroom mirror, studying it, trying to decide if my twelve-year-old self is ugly or pretty. Alexis reassures me constantly that I'm beautiful and I want to believe her, but when I turn to the side I see the bump near the bridge of my nose—the one the boys at school have made fun of, the one I hate. Ugly, I decide. I give up and retreat to my room at the same time that Alexis storms downstairs from her room on the third floor.

"I can't deal with this shit anymore," she says through gritted teeth as she pushes past me in the hallway. She's not talking to me, more of just an angry mumble. She slams the bathroom door. We both have a day off from school and our parents are at work. The bathroom lock clicks as it slides into the strike plate. I hear a rattling sound.

"Lex, are you okay?"

No answer.

"Lex!"

More rattles. It's a familiar sound, but it still takes my brain a couple of beats before it processes the noise: pills being poured out. I know immediately what she is doing. Alexis has kept a suicide journal since she was twelve, in which she wrote down all the times she wanted to die. She's kept the book hidden from my parents, but she showed it to me once.

"Alexis!" I begin pounding on the door, screaming her name, throwing my body against the wood panel over and over before I fall to the floor. This bathroom is where we bathed together as children, where we poured cold water on each other's butts and shrieked in response, where she invented The Periwinkle Club, of which she was, of course, the president. I've seen enough after-school specials about suicide to know about dialing 911, but I do nothing other than lie on the floor crying until I hear the lock slide out of the latch.

"I'm scared," Alexis says. "Will you stay with me?" She is white, ghostly looking.

"Yes."

We go to her room where she falls in and out of alertness, where I slap her face to keep her from losing consciousness.

"Alexis, STAY AWAKE!" I scream. Part of me believes that if I yell loudly enough everything will be okay.

"There's a ringing in my ears," she says, her eyes fluttering shut.

I slap her hard. "WAKE UP!"

"Dani, I'm not gonna die. It's okay." She sounds as if cotton has been stuffed into her mouth. An hour passes this way, maybe two, and slowly she becomes more alert.

"Please Dani, you can't tell Mom or Dad about this."

I hesitate before I answer, but then concede. I've become a masterful secret keeper over the years. "I won't, I promise."

"I have to get out of here," she says. "They'll know something is up." As she throws her black leather jacket over her shoulders, the silver merry-go-round ring tinks against a buckle.

When my parents arrive home, I tell them that Alexis went to Dom's for dinner and I sit with them at the table and eat the food my mother prepares.

"Fine," I say when they ask about my day. When we are done with our meal, I stand at the sink and load the rinsed dishes into the dishwasher.

Years later, Alexis will recall this incident and she will credit her friend, Dom, with saving her life. She will say his name with a kind of reverence. "Dom stayed with me when I needed it most," she will say. "Thank God for Dom."

Second or Third

"ALEXIS IS IN the hospital. She tried to kill herself," my father tells me when he calls.

It's November of 2006 and this is her third attempt, although our parents would say it's the second, since they still don't know about the first time when Alexis was in high school. It will be another ten years, another ten more attempts before she succeeds at taking her life.

"Is she okay?" I'm not sure what I mean when I ask this. Am I asking if she's stable? Brain damaged? Whether she regrets the attempt?

"Yes," he tells me, which makes me feel better even though I have no idea how to interpret it.

The next day I take the day off from my job at a residential remodeling company to drive up to my parents' house to be with them. My own life is in flux. I'm twenty-nine years old, living in a beach town in Delaware in a house I purchased with my partner, whom I've been dating for five years. For the past several months, she and I have been trying to get pregnant using donor sperm, but instead of feeling disappointed by the negative pregnancy tests we've gotten for the last two months, I've found myself feeling relieved and my brain has been working overtime to figure out what the hell this means, even though the answer is laughably obvious. In less than three months, my partner and I will be broken up and we will be trying to sell the house and figure out who will keep our two dogs.

When I arrive home, the details of what happened begin spilling out of my parents, as if they can no longer contain them. They take turns talking. My mother, then my father.

"We found her in her room. She was out of it, but she was still communicating."

"We weren't sure whether we should call an ambulance. We had no idea how much she'd taken. Or what."

"We decided to put her to sleep in the back bedroom so we could hear her if she got up or if she got sick."

"After we went to bed, we heard a noise, so we came to check on her."

"She was on the floor, trying to crawl towards the door. She couldn't even hold her head up."

As I listen, it feels like my body has been carried away on the swift current of their words and I'm struggling to keep my bearings as I'm swept along. Questions begin rising up inside of me: Did they know that this was a suicide attempt, or did they think that my sister was simply high again? Where is the note she left this time? When did they find it? Why didn't they call for help sooner?

I wonder all of these things, but I do not ask. The air is already so thick with guilt and this question would turn the air solid.

My parents lead me upstairs to the room where they found Alexis, and my mother begins acting out what they'd seen, as though the verbal descriptions alone cannot possibly convey the horror.

"She was sprawled here, with her arm stretched out, trying to reach the doorknob."

She mimics the motion Alexis made. She even imitates my sister's facial expression—her eyes half closed, her head lolling to the left and right. She points at the spot on the rug as though my sister is still there, as though there is something that I should be seeing.

I stand, nodding my head. This has become our routine— my parents witness horrific events and then they recount them to me with details so vivid I feel as though I'd witnessed them myself. It used to be that I urged them to share these things with me because I believed that in order to be a part of my family, I needed to be part of the suffering, but over time, the dynamic around this detailed sharing has shifted from a thing I wanted and needed to a thing that weighs me down. I am filled with memories that I had no part in making: my sister strolling naked into the kitchen, putting an empty mug into the microwave to heat up some tea; my sister twitching and convulsing in the waiting room of the ER because she has overdosed on Ritalin. Scenes that I have never actually witnessed have become a part of me.

"Where's the note?" I blurt suddenly, both to stop my parents' ping-ponging, blow-by-blow description of what happened and because I want to see it. To hold it in my hands and read what Alexis thought would be her last words.

Third Attempt Note

Tʜɪѕ ɴᴏᴛᴇ ɪѕ on a yellow Post-it.

> *I'm done. To understand look up Ophelia in Hamlet.*
> *Look up Alice in Wonderland. Look up The Bell Jar.*
> *They are all me. Vincent especially.*
> *I love you.*

Hot anger surges through me, melting everything in its path as I read and re-read her words, looking for things that aren't here—an explanation, an apology. My sister is a writer and this note, scrawled in sloppy handwriting, after the drugs and alcohol had begun to take effect, was all that she thought to leave behind? *This note?* Is this all that we are worth to her? Are we nothing more than an afterthought?

I fold the paper in half twice and slide it into my wallet. I carry it for years before I decide to tuck it away in a box. Suicide seems like the promised end for Alexis, so I make a promise to be ready for it. Every time I see the paper's yellow edge sticking out of my wallet, it's a reminder of her impending death, a glimpse into my future. But it's also a physical object that I can hold in my hand and touch and use to justify my seething anger.

Every time I read the words, I see none of Alexis's pain and suffering, only the wound that this suicide attempt has inflicted on my parents and on me. I scoff at the comparison she's made between herself and Vincent van Gogh, dismissing it as mere narcissism.

Years later, after she is dead, it will occur to me to wonder what she meant by the note. *They are all me.* I will think of Alice, trapped in Wonderland, and the way she was always saying the wrong thing, or drinking or eating something that made her grow or shrink; the way that she found it impossible to fit in. I will read about how van Gogh cut his ear off, not with a sword as I'd always imagined in my cartoonish version of that famous story, but with a razor, and finally, finally my anger over this note will lift. In its place, a deep sympathy for how Alexis felt in the world will settle into me.

Attempt Number _______

MY SHOVEL SINKS into the earth and I push down on the back of the handle to loosen the hard dirt just as my cell phone begins to ring. I'm at my friend Meg's house, helping her plant a row of shrubs along the perimeter of her yard. Meg and her partner Rachel live in a twin home. They have an annoying neighbor and these shrubs are part of the solution to this problem.

"Hey, no phone calls when you're on the clock!" Meg yells to me from across the yard.

"Yes, boss," I say sarcastically. It has become our routine over the years to help one another with home improvement projects. When I needed someone to assist me with hanging drywall after I'd torn out the plaster ceiling in my first home, Meg had come over and worked all day. We'd spent most of it laughing as we struggled to hold the drywall in place before one of us could get a couple of screws into a stud to give us some relief.

I lean the shovel against the fence and pull my phone out of my pocket. I see Alexis's name on the screen and quickly shove the phone back into my sweatshirt. I don't feel like dealing with her today. I grab the shovel and plunge it back into the ground, then deposit a shovelful of dirt into a pile about a foot away from the hole.

"How deep do I need to make this?" I holler to Meg, who is standing with her hands on her hips. Meg is an inch taller than my 5'7" frame, but she is built like a bull. Her curly black hair is tied in the customary low ponytail that she frequently wears. She turns my way and glares before dissolving into laughter. "How the hell would I know?" she says.

My phone rings again. Alexis. *Shit*, I think. If she's calling me two times in a row, something is wrong.

"Hello?"

"Dani? I need to ask you a question..." She's slurring. "Sylvia Plath," she says. "Did she just put her head in the oven? Is that what she did? Just put her head in the oven and bake it like a hamburger?"

In the yard, I hear Meg sigh dramatically and say, "Good help is so hard to find," but I plug my ear to block her out and the whole world telescopes into one singular point of focus. I walk away from the hole I've just dug, heading toward the house where it will be quiet. "Lex, what's going on? Are you okay?"

"I cut my wrist and there's blood. A lot of blood. I tried cleaning up a little, but did she? Did she just put her head in the oven? Is that what she did?"

Inside the house, I stand at the counter, leaning against it for support, trying to figure out what to do. Alexis is in her apartment in Philly. I'm in Baltimore.

"Lex, I'm going to call you right back, okay? You promise me that you'll answer when I call back, okay?"

"Yeah, but I just want to know about Sylvia Plath..."

"PROMISE ME you'll answer!"

"I promise, Dani."

I hang up and dial my parents in the hope that they are on their way to her apartment. My father picks up.

"Have you talked to Alexis?"

"Yeah," he says. "About a half an hour ago. We're packing up now to leave from Cape May to go to her apartment."

"You're down the shore? You have a two-hour drive before you get to her apartment. Did you call 911?"

"We can't call 911 from here," he says. "It'll just go through to the Cape May operator."

"Jesus Christ! Just call the Philadelphia police."

I hang up on him, ever aware of the minutes that have ticked by since I got off the phone with Alexis. I dial Lindsay. "I need your help," I blurt out when she answers. "I need you to look up the number for the Philadelphia police and send them to my sister's apartment. She's trying to kill herself. Please. I need to call her back to make sure she's okay."

"What's the address?" she asks calmly.

I give it to her, then hang up and call Alexis's number.

"Hey," she says sleepily when she answers.

"Lex? How you doing?"

"I'm 'kay."

"What'd you do to your wrist?"

"I cut it. It's talking to me, looking at me."

"Can you wrap it up?" I ask. "Maybe you should wrap it up."

"Hmm...did did did she just put it in the oven, Sylvia Plath?"

"I don't know," I say. "Did you take any pills?"

"Did she just, um, just bake it like a hamburger?"

"I don't know. How many pills did you take?"

"It's staring at me. Like an eye."

"Wrap it up. It'll feel better if you wrap it up."

I hear a loud banging on the door.

"Go answer the door," I tell her. "Someone is at your door."

"Huh? The door?"

"Yes, go answer the door."

"Okay."

The phone drops to the floor, and then I hear the voices of two men, then my sister's voice breaking into tears. "I didn't call you. Why are you here? I didn't call."

I listen for a few more minutes as she wails in protest at whatever they are doing and then I hang up and call my parents back.

"Hello?" my mother answers.

"I called 911," I say. "The paramedics just got there."

"What'd you do that for?" my mother snaps.

Her words stun me even though I know exactly why she is upset. Alexis will be taken to the hospital, stabilized, and then admitted to a psych ward. Nearly all of the psych wards that she's ever been to have been poorly-run, filthy messes, and that is where I have just sent her.

I call Lindsay to tell her that the paramedics arrived and to thank her.

"You okay?" she asks.

"No."

"You staying there?"

"Yeah, there's nothing else I can do right now."

I go back outside and pick up my shovel and plunge it deep into the earth, happy to have the physical labor as an outlet. Normally, I would go for a run to calm my nerves. I would let my feet slap the earth and I would push my body hard, in a way that borders on punishment, and I would relish the pain. In these moments, the pain brings me back to center. I have failed my sister in some essential way and demanding difficult things from my body feels good. My shovel clangs against a rock and I move it to the left, stab it down again, and then wedge it underneath the stone for leverage. I pull hard, but the spade slips off the rock, sending the sound of metal scraping stone through the yard.

Meg is next to me suddenly. "Is everything okay?" she asks gently.

I shake my head no. "My sister," I start, but can't finish.

Meg puts her hand on my shoulder. Meg has two siblings who struggle with addiction. Her brother is still in active addiction, but her sister has several years of sobriety under her belt after kicking a heroin addiction that nearly killed her. The two of them have started to mend their relationship, which leaves me both with a sense of wonder and hope. Sometimes I pepper Meg with questions about how she has found a way to trust her sister again. Meg knows what it feels like to have a sibling skirt death again and again; knows the feelings of helplessness and anger and fear.

"Do you want to talk about it?"

"No."

"Good," she says, "because these shrubs aren't going to plant themselves."

I laugh, grateful for the release and for Meg. Laughter is a throughline in our friendship. No matter how much either of us is suffering, we both have the ability to make the other laugh. "You're such an ass," I say as I jab the shovel down again next to the stone. With one hard jerk of the handle, I wrench it loose.

Several days later, after my parents find out that Alexis had turned on the gas from the stove in her apartment, my mother calls and apologizes to me. "I'm sorry I got upset with you for calling 911," she says. "I didn't know that Alexis had the gas on. She could've blown up the whole building."

Busy Day

"SEE YOU IN a couple of days," I say to Lindsay outside of my parents' house, the day after we learned that Alexis was dead. "I love you." I feel like a frayed wire going in several directions, currents pulsing through me with no circuit to complete.

"Love you too," she says, squeezing me tight. "D, are you sure you don't need me to stay?" I hesitate a moment. My parents and I have a day of appointments ahead of us: the priest, the undertaker, the cemetery. Part of me wants her by my side as I go through the logistics of planning a funeral for the first time in my life, but a bigger part of me wants her to leave, both to spare her from such a heavy burden and because I don't want to have to consider another set of feelings and needs—whether she is hungry, tired, annoyed. Also, shooing her away allows me to hold on to the pretense that I can handle all of this, which I'm not actually sure is true.

"No, I'll be okay. We're going to be running around all day. When we figure things out, we can decide when you should come back."

"Okay, call me later."

I wave to Lindsay as she drives away. As soon as she is out of sight, I wish that I'd told her to stay. My father and mother emerge from the house and we all get into the car. My father's brow is already covered with sweat on this unusually warm May day and he puts the air conditioner on full blast. As we pull out of their development, the seat belt reminder dings.

"Dad, please put on your seat belt," I say. It's strange to hear this coming out of my mouth. It's a thing I've been saying to him since high school, but it feels old and new at once. Things are the same, but nothing is the same.

We pull into the parking lot at St. Phil's, across from the old bus yard where Alexis hung out with her beloved skaters. I look around at our elementary school and remember the day that Alexis bought me a cupcake from the bake sale and presented it to me as we waited in line for the bus. She'd held it out on the palm of her hand and sung happy birthday to me, even though my birthday wasn't until August. When she finished, she smashed it in my face. I burst into tears, both out of embarrassment and bafflement over why she would do that to me. But that was just how she was, a blend of cruelty and kindness mixed together. She'd do something awful during the day and then invite me into her room that same night to read to me. When I entered my teen years, she constantly told me that I was beautiful because she knew how wildly self-conscious I felt in my body, but if I pissed her off she'd call me "Beaker" because she knew how insecure I was about the pointiness of my nose, and she knew that this name would cut me to the bone.

At the church rectory, we are ushered into a room with a large wooden dining table and told that Father Steve will be with us shortly. The room is packed with holiday decorations. In the corner, there's a fake Christmas tree with a dusty tree skirt beneath it. A stuffed Easter Bunny wearing a crooked

Santa hat is propped on a cluttered chest next to a creepy-looking fake arm, the kind people shut in a door around Halloween.

My eyes sweep over the piles of seasonal junk, wondering why there's not a more appropriate meeting room. If they have no other place to store these decorations, at the very least they could drape sheets over them so that grieving families don't have to stare at a fake dismembered arm. Even my vet's office is more thoughtful when it comes to the newly bereaved. There, they keep a candle on the front desk next to a sign that asks people to please speak quietly when the candle is lit because it means that someone is inside a nearby room saying goodbye to an animal. This room strikes me as both completely tone-deaf and perfectly emblematic of a church that preaches love and honesty yet covers up its own sexual abuse scandals.

Father Steve enters briskly. "I'm so sorry for your loss," he says as he extends his right hand and places his left hand on top of each of ours as we shake. His movements are brisk and businesslike. My opinion of him is already tainted from his earlier childish demonstration of spitefulness with the funeral director from Riley's, but the moment I see him I decide with certainty that Alexis would not have liked him, and I therefore feel it is my job to display some sort of hostility toward him, or at the very least to refrain from being nice. Alexis was, like me, a lapsed Catholic, or as I sometimes joke, a recovering one. We'd both come to look at the Catholic faith as a thing that had scarred us with its heavy doses of guilt. She'd quit going to church on Sundays long before me.

Father Steve sits down at the head of the table, passes each of us a large hardcover book, and directs us to open it to page 274. I keep waiting for him to explain the bizarre décor or at the very least apologize for it, but he says nothing.

The book is full of readings appropriate for numerous

occasions: death of a parent, death of a child. I suppose this is efficient, but it feels incredibly insensitive and generic. Father Paul acts as a seasoned guide, pointing out readings that he likes to use for funerals. His suggestions are full of talk of eternal life, so I begin skipping ahead, skimming for ones that read more like poetry, knowing that would be what Alexis wanted—words that mean something.

"I think she would like this," I say, pointing to a reading from the Book of Wisdom that says, "The souls of the dead shall be touched by no torment... They seemed in the view of the foolish, to be dead; and their passing away was thought an affliction and their going forth from us utter destruction. But they are at peace." In actuality, maybe I am the one who likes it, mostly because of the last line. I desperately want to believe that she is at peace.

To my relief, Father Steve doesn't ask how Alexis died. Deep in the recesses of my mind, I recall learning that the Catholic church viewed suicide as the ultimate sin, a slap in the face to the God who had bestowed life. I have no idea whether this remains a teaching of the church, but I don't want to find out. What I'd like to do is give the finger to God and scream that my sister hadn't had any kind of life.

Once we select the readings, Father Steve tries to lead us through the hymns and, again, I ignore his ideas. We choose *On Eagle's Wings* and *Ave Maria* but we need another. I flip to the index to find *Lord of the Dance*. As kids, whenever Alexis and I were bored at Sunday mass, she'd instruct me to open my hymnal and we'd sit hunched on the pew, quietly singing to each other. I don't know why she chose that song, or where she learned it, but it quickly became familiar to me, and it felt like a secret we shared.

"Let's do this one," I say, pointing to it. My parents lean over to see the page number.

"I don't know that one," my dad says.

"Lex and I used to sing it together..."

"What number?" Father Steve asks.

"205," I say and he jots it down.

"I'll need some other things from you," he says. He pushes his glasses up off the end of his nose, but they slide right back down because of the way he tilts his head to look out over them. "I'll need some information about Alexis, so that I can personalize the homily. I like to do that, you know."

I scribble this on the notepad I've brought with me. I've taken it upon myself to try to handle as much of the logistical aspects as possible because it seems like neither my mother nor father are equipped to do it, and because it's a relief for me to have some sort of tangible way to help.

"Also, if you'd like to personalize the responsorial psalm, you may do that." He hands me a paper with the standard psalm.

"What about a eulogy?" I ask.

"Well, I don't allow them during the mass," he says. "I used to, but I've had a string of bad experiences. Once, I had a man come up and tell a bunch of fishing stories. When he was finished, he cracked open a beer, took a swig, and said 'We're going to f-ing miss you.'" Father Steve mimics the motion that the man must have made, raising his arm up. "Then he slammed the beer on the altar!" His voice goes up at the end of the sentence, as if he is surprised even in the retelling.

It takes real effort for me to refrain from rolling my eyes, but I feel that I've already pushed some invisible limit by brushing off Father Steve's suggested readings, and I don't want to risk angering him and giving him a reason to assert his power. When Alexis and I attended grade school here, our classes were trained to stand any time a priest entered the room and greet him in unison. From the moment Father Steve walked into the room I've been keenly aware that the best way to get what I want from him is by being deferential and polite, so I've been curtsying like a young child at a performance, even as I've been trying to be passively defiant, like a slouching, uninterested teen.

I glance over at my parents to gauge their reaction to his beer story, but their expressions reveal nothing of their emotions. "Well, I don't think you need to worry about anyone in our group slamming beers on the altar," I say, flashing a fake smile. He nods.

"If you want to do something before the mass begins, I will allow that," he says. "Some priests don't allow anything, but I do."

"That works," I say.

"And who will be doing it?"

"Alexis's friend Michelle." I pause. "And maybe me."

Tinnitus

IT'S EASTER SUNDAY of 2015, a beautiful spring day—one of the first after a long, snowy winter—and I call home to wish my family a happy Easter.

My father answers. "Hi Dani," he says happily.

"Hey Pops, what are you up to?"

I have my hands-free device plugged into my ears and my phone tucked into my back pocket, so I can clean the bathroom as we talk. We chit-chat easily and I wipe down the counters and mirrors, then I grab the drain snake—a Tommy-gun-shaped device that's used to clear clogs in the shower. Fifteen minutes before, I'd been outside soaking up the nice weather and raking leaves that we'd neglected in the fall, when Lindsay called to me from the back door, saying that she thought the leaves could wait, and could we please concentrate on the inside of our house. In response, I'd gotten annoyed that she didn't appreciate the work that I was doing and huffed inside, stomping upstairs like a sullen teen.

"Mom's all excited because Little Billy and Kathy are coming over with the kids and we're going to have an egg hunt. She's got all these plastic eggs all over the place." He laughs. "Oh boy. She's busy cooking now."

I know without asking that she's making ham, carrots, potatoes, and manicotti. I can taste my mom's manicotti—the delicate, homemade crepes that she fills with ricotta cheese—and I feel intensely homesick all at once.

"Do you want to talk to Lex?" my dad asks.

If I were to answer honestly I would say no, but in my family politeness always trumps honesty.

"Sure," I say.

"Hey Dani," she says after my dad passes the phone to her. "Happy Easter. How are you?"

I do my best to think of an answer that includes a benign detail of my life that sounds like something significant, but reveals nothing about my actual life, the sort of thing I'd tell a stranger. Nothing comes to mind.

"I'm good, just doing a little cleaning. How are you?"

She begins cruising down a litany of woes and relief floods my system as I realize that this is going to be one of the conversations where she does most of the talking. These are the most effortless in that they require little from me other than the occasional noise to indicate I'm still listening. The latest problem, according to Alexis, is a loud and obtrusive ringing in her ears. "It's so loud I can't stand it," she says. "My doctor says it's definitely not tinnitus." She starts crying. "If it doesn't stop, I might have to go to the ER today."

Easter Sunday in the ER, I think. My father will be tasked with taking Alexis to the hospital since she doesn't drive and my mom will be busy getting dinner ready. An image of my father flashes through my mind. In it, he nods off in the uncomfortable ER chairs, his arms crossed over his big belly, his head rolling forward, startling him awake, his grey hair lit up by a beam of sunlight, a whistling snore escaping from his long nose.

I recall a blur of other holidays: the Christmas my sister

slipped a belt around her neck when my mother refused to give her the medication she'd been abusing, the Easter she had a seizure after we'd finished dinner. That year, I'd ridden in the ambulance with her on the way to the ER and she kept thanking me, looking up at me with her big, green eyes.

She's sick, I tell myself in the hopes that this will banish my anger, cause it to evaporate into an invisible haze, but my head pounds when I think back on these instances. I take a deep breath through my nose.

"I'm sorry," I say to her. "That sounds awful, Lex." I'm always saying things like this when we are on the phone. *I bet that's tough*, I'll say, or *I'm sorry*, or *uh-huh*. My inflection is the same every time, but my voice is consistently devoid of any emotion.

I unscrew the shower cleanout and pull a long spring from the drain snake. I push the coil down until it hits something, then wiggle it until it goes a few more inches. When I can't get it to move any more, I lock the spring in place with a small set screw and begin to spin the handle around and around.

"I've googled about tinnitus," Alexis says.

"Uh-huh," I say.

"The ringing could be a side effect of my Zyprexa, but I stopped taking that and started Risperdal, but maybe I'm having seizures or maybe it's my Cavernoma." She continues on like this, her voice a half-mumble, telling me about the different possible causes.

In my hand, the drain snake becomes harder to spin, which means that it's driving into the clog of hair. I keep turning. The spring jerks like a writhing fish, clanging against the cleanout as tension builds in the line.

I've come to see my sister as a cartoon-like character, someone akin to Wile E. Coyote, who always ends up with an anvil dropping on his head or a stick of dynamite going off in his hand—comedic pratfalls of the most sordid kind.

When the coyote inevitably runs off a cliff, I never think about what he would look like after falling; never conjure an image of his body, bloodied and broken at the bottom. If I thought about that, I wouldn't be able to watch that show. It's the same with my sister.

Later today I will go online and google tinnitus. Among its many causes, I will find that it can be linked to withdrawing from Benzodiazepine and I will think, *Aha, I've found it.* Then, there will be a voice in my head that will scold me for assuming the worst about her. *What if you're wrong? What if it's not from drugs? What if it's just some fluke and she's suffering through no fault of her own and you can't muster up one goddamned ounce of empathy?*

"You think that's it?" I ask in response to one of her theories.

I tug on the spring, but it doesn't budge, so I turn it back a couple of turns and tug again. With effort, it moves an inch out of the cleanout. I pull again and it gives. I draw the long spring out.

At the end, a stinking mass of wet brown hair, slick with soap, is twisted and dangling. It drips black sludge onto the porcelain.

A couple of years ago, my sister wound up in the hospital unconscious after some sort of seizure. For an entire week, she didn't wake up and the doctors who came in and out of her room consulted with my mother, father, and me about her treatment regimen. We got to make all of the decisions regarding her care, and I had the rare experience of knowing that she wasn't doing or taking anything to muck up the works; that she couldn't get in the way of her own best interest, and in the strangest way, this made it so easy for me to be a loving sister.

When she finally woke up after a week, I was elated, but soon realized that it meant that the doctors no longer needed to consult us about her care and I felt an immediate sense of helplessness followed by a roaring wave of anger. If I couldn't control her, I didn't know how to love her.

"I just wish it would stop," she says.

"I know, Lex. Me too."

I look at the chunk of tangled hair. I force myself to touch it so that I can begin unwinding it from the spring.

Sister-in-Law

LINDSAY IS ALWAYS polite to Alexis, always hugs her hello and goodbye, buys her Christmas presents—but it's a formal, stiff relationship; one that exists only because of the connection each has to me. This isn't something that Lindsay and I discuss, it's simply understood.

Lindsay has seen too many awful things happen: it was she who was with me the night that Alexis cut her wrist and knocked on our bedroom door; she who heard my sister call me a bitch for waking my parents and suggesting we call 911; she who held my quivering body later that night when things had settled down; she who has so many times picked up the pieces of my broken psyche after visits home or phone calls with my sister.

Part of me revels in Lindsay's dislike because it validates my own negative feelings toward Alexis. I figure that if my rational, reasonable, kind wife can't find any redeeming traits in my sister, then maybe I'm not as bad a person as I've come to believe.

I am totally unprepared for the way that my feelings will

change the moment Alexis dies, and a long-blurred version of her comes speeding into sharp focus: Alexis fixing my hair for school pictures; Alexis holding me in her arms the day that I tearfully came out to her; Alexis inviting me to parties when I was a lonely and awkward teen; Alexis helping me get my first job out of college.

Along with these versions of my sister, the strangest set of desires will spring up inside me. Chief among these will be the desire for Lindsay to like my sister, to *love* my sister. I will yearn for Lindsay to look at me with a wistful smile and tell me a story she recalls about Alexis that isn't tinged with some dark shadow. But she will have none and this lack will separate us.

I don't need your protection anymore, I want to tell her, but I won't be able to find the words and she won't be able to relinquish her vigilance, as if Alexis could wound me in death more than she ever could when she was alive.

I will rarely speak longingly for my sister, but when I do, I will feel the static edges of Lindsay's fear floating out in the air around us, as if she's afraid that I will be swallowed whole by my guilt if I forget all of the terrible things that happened when Alexis was alive, and she might be right. I will both love and loathe her for this.

Now

For years Lindsay said she wanted to marry me, but "not now."

"Of course I want to marry *you*, but I'm not ready," she'd tell me. "I know you're my person, so what's the rush?"

To which I'd reply, "If you know, why wait? What are we waiting for?"

We must've had a hundred variations of that conversation right up until we got married, five years into our relationship. By that time, it felt like I'd been running in place and I'd exhausted my store of patience.

Once we got married, Lindsay's "not now" shifted to wanting a baby, and once again I felt as though I could see our future life, but could do nothing to move toward it. Years passed this way with my love for Lindsay pressed right up against my yearning for a family that she was simply not ready for.

Threads of resentment stitched their way so tightly around my heart that by the time Lindsay began to shift away from the "not now"—coming home to tell me about how cute her coworkers' kids were—our relationship felt hemmed shut by my resentment. Finally, *she* was ready, but *we* felt disconnected from one another. We couldn't communicate through the simplest disagreements. Arguments erupted over the tone of voice that one or the other of us used when expressing frustration over the dishes in the sink or any other number of inane annoyances inherent in a marriage.

It didn't help that I had carried a hefty load of baggage from my previous long-term relationship right into my current one. In my past relationship, I had been the one who dragged my feet in a way that now felt eerily similar to Lindsay—first at the prospect of getting married and then later at the prospect of kids. At the time, I hadn't known what caused my extreme hesitancy, but in hindsight I'd come to understand that even though my ex was a perfectly lovely woman, there was something lacking in our relationship, and it was this missing thing that kept me from fully committing. We'd stayed together for five years because I'd been too afraid to leave a good thing simply because "something" had been missing; because good was not enough. I worried the same might be true for Lindsay.

The week before my sister died, Lindsay and I sat on the couch in our living room, our two dogs nestled on the rug. After months of agonizing, I finally felt clear on what I needed to do. I'd talked to my therapist and spent hours and hours contemplating what I was about to say, because I knew that it could end our relationship.

"I don't think I can be happy if we never try to have a baby," I said. "If we try and it doesn't happen, I think I could be okay, but if we never try, I'll resent it and that resentment will only grow. I might be okay. I might find other things to throw myself into—maybe even volunteer with Big Brothers Big Sisters or something, but I just don't know. I don't think that'll be enough."

Lindsay sat quietly, as if trying to absorb what I'd said.

Would she see this as an ultimatum? Was it? She did not typically respond well to that type of pressure.

"Well," she said after what felt like an eternity, "then let's start the process."

And so we did. Just like that. We made an appointment with a fertility center the following day.

One week later, Alexis was dead.

Five months later, Lindsay was pregnant.

Reaching

AT SIXTEEN ALEXIS begins hanging out with a group of skaters at the old bus yard across from her elementary school—a broken-down parking lot of cracked concrete. On Sundays, this same lot overflows with the vehicles of dutiful Catholics poised to check church off of the to-do list. Each week when our family arrives at the lot in our father's burgundy Caprice Classic, a company car, there's always the inevitable dip of a tire into a pothole, followed by the scraping of metal, followed by our father's angry voice goddamning this goddamn lot, followed by our mother saying, "Nick, we're on our way to church."

This period with the skaters is one that Alexis looks back on wistfully for the rest of her life. During college, Alexis writes an essay called *Death of the Bus Yard*, where she chronicles the impact this time had on her. In the opening line she writes, "It began with a cat call. One of those 'fweet fweow' whistles from one of the nameless skateboarders in the darkened lot."

She describes the way that she and her friend, bored by the prospect of watching another movie, had gone out walking around their small town. The two of them slowed down in response to the whistle, tentatively waiting for what might come next.

"How 'bout them Knicks?" one of the boys called, his voice "low and scratchy, like a piece of taut satin pulled over a cactus." That was how it began.

And so the pockmarked lot that my father despises becomes the place Alexis feels most at ease in her teenage years. The bus yard is her refuge. At dinner each night she argues with our mother and father. Explosive fights over where she will apply to college. They want her to apply to St. Joseph's University, where our mother works and the tuition would be free. But our father had always promised her that she could go to school wherever she wanted, and now suddenly when the time has arrived, they are pressuring her to go where it will be free so that they will not have to go into massive debt.

"I am not applying to St. Joe's," she screams during these arguments. She knows if she applies that she'll be accepted, maybe even get offered a scholarship, and when that happens, she won't be able to hold her ground against the flood of reasons pushing in that direction. Most fights end with her mother calling her an ingrate and her father calling her selfish. She runs upstairs without finishing her dinner and throws herself on her bed and weeps.

At the bus yard she feels free. All the skaters trade stories about their asshole parents. They wish they were eighteen, they say, they'll move out as soon as they turn eighteen. She feels a sense of belonging when she's there unlike anything she's ever experienced. When she can't make it to hang out, the boys tell her how much they missed her. She loves watching them skate back and forth over the entrance ramp, the only part that's still relatively smooth. On either side of the ramp's opening there are perfectly formed slopes where the skaters take turns trying to impress each other with tricks. They smoke cigarettes and curse. When they get cold, they pull their arms into the sleeves of their shirts and ball up their hands into fists. They are, each in their own way, misunderstood.

Terry is Alexis's favorite of the skater boys. He has wiry hair and a boisterous laugh, and calls everybody "jaunski." "*What's up jaunski,*" he yells whenever someone arrives at the bus yard. Terry kisses her one night in the back corner of the large lot, near a wall where someone has spray-painted a hand with an extended middle finger.

There are enough constants at the bus yard to allow a sense of familiarity and comfort to develop—the sound of the skateboards on the cement, the plumes of smoke that rise above them when they sit in a circle, the ivy that has grown up the chain link fence that surrounds the lot, the way they sit and rock side to side on the boards when they talk. All these things are the same each time they gather, and it feels like home to her.

Which is why it is so devastating to her when the township comes in one day with bulldozers and heavy equipment to repave the cratered old lot. In its place, a smooth blacktop surface with neat lines of parking spots is created. She writes that, "The destruction of the bus-yard marked the end of the comfortable period in my life. My circle of friends slowly fell apart. Someone stole our teenage playground and we were forced to grow up."

The very first time that Alexis shared this essay with me, I was simultaneously impressed and stung with jealousy over her mastery of words. To this day, the descriptions in *Death of the Bus Yard* remain some of the best I've ever read. In one section she compares the sound of skateboard wheels on cement to pool balls being poured over a sheet of glass.

After Alexis dies, I reread this essay and feel the same awe from all those years ago. She ends the essay with this: "I moved into my senior year and decided to go away to college. After that, the decisions became even harder, and as I further move into adulthood, I know more demons await me."

Cleanup Crew

THERE ARE NIGHTLY fights at the dinner table about where Alexis will go to college. Most of these end with Alexis storming upstairs in tears. Some days I follow Alexis to her room and stroke her hair and listen to her vent about how she wishes she could just be at the bus yard, about how unfair our parents are being, about how they are such assholes. Other times I stay with my mother and father. I sit there moving food around, listening to them letting out long sighs and clanking their utensils against their plates. My rule of thumb is to tend to whoever seems the most wounded. At thirteen, I've already learned the art of triage.

I've become a kind of one-woman cleanup crew picking up pieces after an argument, finding the right mix of behaviors to counteract the intensity. Sometimes I crack jokes. Other times I tell a story—anything to help settle the dust. Today I take on the role of deferential daughter.

"I'll never fight with you like that," I say to my parents. My father looks up at me from his fettuccini noodles. Whenever we have pasta, he holds his spoon under his fork and twirls the noodles into manageable bites. He says that's the way real Italians do it. He doesn't do anything else the way real Italians do, so I'm not sure why he stresses this every time we eat pasta.

"You won't, huh?"

"Nope. I'll go to school wherever you want." My father looks amused. "I promise." I can see he doesn't believe me, so I keep going. "I mean, St. Joe's is a great school. You went there. And I already love going to the basketball games." I can see that I've got his attention now. "You used to go to the games when you went there, right? What's that story about when the Hawks would play the Georgetown team? What was their mascot?" I already know the story about the way that the students from the two schools would antagonize each other over their respective mascots, but I know that he loves telling it.

"The Hoya," he tells me, perking up a bit. "They'd yell, 'The Hawk is dead. The Hawk is dead.' And we'd yell, 'What the hell's a Hoya? What the hell's a Hoya?'" He always smiles when he tells this story and tonight is no different. Mission accomplished.

The Names She Called Me

WHEN WE WERE kids, she called me Beaker because my nose was pointy, like a bird's beak.

"Shut up," I'd scream at her.

"Oh, okay. I'll shut up, Beaker. Sorry about that, Beaker."

She begged my parents to name me Bobby after the youngest brother on *The Brady Bunch* when I was born, but my parents named me after my mother's dead brother, Danny.

"I call you the Tin Man," she said during a phone conversation, "because you have no heart."

Once, as she was getting out of my car, she hugged me and said, "You're a good sister." I'd just bought her a fancy coffee at Starbucks before dropping her off at the hospital to visit our cousin who was on life support after a drug overdose. I'd been there the previous day to witness the ventilator jerking his chest up for each breath.

"Sometimes," I sighed in response. She smiled, then hugged me before she got out of the car and I watched her make her way through the automated sliding doors. The very next week, she would be in the same hospital after having a strange seizure.

"Little bitch" was what she called me after I suggested then urged my parents to call 911 on the Thanksgiving night she cut her wrist.

"Bitch," she'd screamed, her eyes on fire. "You're a little bitch."

At some point growing up, she began calling me Dani. For a long time, she was the only one who called me this, and I felt special whenever she said it. When I went to her with a problem, she would hug me and say, "It'll be okay, Dani." Then she'd briskly rub my head and mess up my hair.

In her suicide note she wrote: "Tell Dani I love her."

The Undertaker

WHEN MY PARENTS and I arrive at Riley's funeral home, we take an elevator up to the offices. The elevator is carpeted with the same pattern as my parents' old dining room rug, which strikes me as such an odd coincidence that I feel compelled to point it out. It's the same compulsion I feel whenever Lindsay and I are watching T.V. and I see an actor from some long-ago series playing a role in *NCIS*. "Hey, that's Jane from *Melrose Place*!" I'll say as soon as I make the connection, unable to hold this knowledge without sharing it. My parents nod, unimpressed, and I feel immediately foolish for acknowledging such a mundane detail. A woman steps out from an office when she hears the doors open.

"I'm Brigid. Please, come in." Brigid is overly tan with straight auburn hair and deep-set, blazing blue eyes. She has a hard look about her—a look I associate with women who ride motorcycles.

There are only two chairs for guests in her office, so she goes scurrying off to look for a third. She smiles when she returns with it.

"How's Erin?" my mom asks Brigid. As I listen, I gather that Erin Riley is Brigid's sister who attended St. Joseph's University. Erin has lost not one, but three of her young children—first a boy, then two girls—some years back. I wonder how the universe can be so cruel and how this Erin woman could've survived such a thing. Next week, Lindsay and I have our first appointment scheduled at the fertility center, which will be the start of our journey to becoming pregnant. The idea of motherhood still feels far off—Lindsay will need to go through a series of tests and we'll need to choose a sperm donor—but it also feels closer and more real than ever before. This new proximity to motherhood has allowed me to imagine this whole loss through my own mother's eyes.

"Erin's not involved in the business," Brigid tells my mom, "but she has a flower shop. She does all of our arrangements." She pauses. "So, do we know what we want the obituary to say?" *The obituary*, I think, *my sister's obituary*.

"I want a picture," my mother says immediately. We spend the next ten minutes deciding who should be named as surviving relatives and whether we want to request that donations be made in Alexis's memory. My mother mentions a quote that she's read in other obituaries, but she can't remember exactly what it is. "Something about being kind because you don't know what people have going on," she says. I grab my phone and start googling, happy for a distraction.

"What do you want to do for a mass card? Do you want a prayer on it or a picture of Alexis, or both?" Brigid asks. I think of the old mass cards my mother saved from funerals, tucked behind the frame of her makeup mirror. For years, she had one from her brother Danny's funeral that had the lyrics to *Danny Boy* written on the back. Now I will have one for my sister.

"Oh, I think I found it," I say. "'Everyone you know is fighting a battle you know nothing about. Be kind always.'"

"Yeah, that's it," my mom says.

Brigid pulls out a three-ring binder full of pages of old cards that are slid into clear plastic slots. It reminds me of the books I used as a kid to collect baseball cards. I wonder whether Alexis's card will wind up in here. Whether some other bereaved family will page through this book and see my sister's face.

As we ponder each option, a blonde woman walks briskly into the office and hugs my mom. "Clare, I'm so sorry." She has the same blue eyes as Brigid, and my mother swallows back her tears when she introduces the woman to my father and me as Erin. Erin has freckles sprinkled across the bridge of her nose. I study her carefully, looking for signs of the loss she's dealt with. This is a thing I'll find myself doing every time I meet someone who has lost a child, looking for clues as to what to expect from my parents in the coming weeks, months, years. I wish there was a book similar to the one I'm holding in my hands that could lay out in pictures what their grief will look like. The uncertainty has me on edge.

"Erin, how did you do it? How did you get through it?" my mother asks.

"Clare, moment by moment."

With Erin in the room, the decisions feel easier. When Brigid asks if we want to see Alexis before she's cremated, my parents look to Erin for help. She shakes her head no.

"She won't look like herself," she says. "The blood would've pooled in her face, since she was found face down."

Brigid hands my mother a brochure with photos of marble urns. My father and I peer at it over her shoulder and go back and forth over colors—traditional white, navy, black—before the answer strikes me.

"Red!" I say. "She'd want something bright. She loved being the center of attention." We all laugh, knowing how true this is. Red it would be.

Collecting

ALEXIS AND I race to be the first to reach a pinecone just ahead of us. She gets there first, grabs it, waves it in my face, and then runs back to our mother, presenting it to her as if it's a golden egg. My four-year-old self is indignant at this injustice, and I stomp my foot. "No fair. I saw it first."

Alexis is already running ahead of us again. My mother bends down and zips my coat. "Do you want your hat?" she asks. I shake my head. "There are plenty more just up ahead, honey. Look." She points and I see how many small brown dots speckle the green grass up ahead.

We're walking along the edge of St. Peter and Paul Cemetery, just inside its iron gate, which is flanked by tall pines. We've come to collect the pinecones that my mother uses to make homemade wreaths around the holidays. My father catches up to us and grabs my mother's hand. "You'd better hurry," he says to me.

I sprint away, passing Alexis, who has bent over to tie her shoe. She straightens up as I whiz by and begins chasing after me. Before long, she passes me again. She's faster, stronger, more developed. The sight of her from behind will be a view I become accustomed to throughout my childhood and into young adulthood.

As we grow up, I will stand on the sidelines watching jealously as she leaves for sleepovers, goes out on dates with boyfriends, heads off to college, lands her first job. I will develop an impatience that will stay with me, a habit of rushing through things in the hopes that I might catch up to her. When I look at Alexis I will see the future I hope for. I'll come to believe that if I step in the tracks she has left behind, our lives will lay out identically.

It will come as a surprise to both of us when I stop my mad scramble to catch up with her during my freshman year of college. I'll look at the path she's chosen and I will turn in the exact opposite direction. I'll believe that this pivot means that I've begun to forge my own identity. But what I'll fail to understand is that this turning away also centers around her; that I continue to define myself in relation to her.

Still, the shift will hurt her in a way that neither of us will ever name. Having me trail behind her was affirmation that her life was a thing worthy of repeating and when I stop, it will be a blow to her fragile sense of self—a thing I can't help, but a thing I will always feel like I should apologize for.

Just ahead of me, Alexis reaches the spot my mother pointed to and begins picking up pinecones, holding them in the crook of her arm. I do the same, dropping one each time I tuck one away. She looks at me gleefully.

"I have more," she says. "I win." She runs back to my mother and I watch her long hair trail behind her in the crisp fall air.

Sisters

I RIDE DOWN to the train station with my father and wait anxiously for Alexis, who is coming home for a weekend visit. We've both recently started our freshman years, hers at college, mine in high school. When I spot her coming through the doors, I jump out of the car and nearly tackle her, throwing my arms around her neck and squeezing. I breathe a long sigh of relief and tell her it's good to see her. She laughs and hugs me back.

"Oh my God, you've gotten taller than me," she says. I let go and see that she is right. When I look at her, I am looking down for the first time.

This surprises me because it feels like my feet are the only part of my body in any sort of rush to develop. It seems that they've morphed overnight into size tens. They stick out from the end of my scrawny chicken legs and the only consolation is the fact that they make it difficult to knock me over on the soccer field. By some miracle, I made the freshman team. When I go to practice every day, I listen to the other girls complain about how they're "on the rag" and laugh as they share stories about how far they've gone with their boyfriends—things that seem a long time off from ever happening to me. I am quiet and painfully shy, except for an occasional wry remark that comes out of my mouth when I am feeling brave enough.

When Alexis went away to college, I felt abandoned. Since she left I've spent my time in emotional fits—sometimes stewing over the fact that she wouldn't be around to see me off to proms or watch me grow up; other times crying because I miss her so much. I've taken to doing my homework in her bedroom. Alexis and I talk on the phone, but it's not the same. She's busy with her new boyfriend, James, and trying to adjust to eating at "the caf," as they call it at her school. When my mother gets on the phone with her, she always asks what my sister ate for dinner and then hollers something like "That's all starch!" after my sister tells her. I send Alexis letters in the mail, signing them "Love Always" and then tucking a five or ten-dollar bill between the pages. "Have a beer or two on me," I write, feeling cool. I get the money from my grandparents who are always slipping me ten or twenty dollars.

When we arrive home from the train station, the phone begins ringing as we eat dinner, which highlights the stark contrast between my nonexistent social life and hers. My sister's friends call one after another. The two of us scarf down our food and rush upstairs to her room so we can catch up. I sit on the floor and listen as she makes plans for the night. In between calls, she fills me in on the latest happenings in her life. She's in love with James, but he is a die-hard Republican and they fight a lot. She says he listens to someone called Rush Limbaugh, who I've never heard of. She shows me her fake ID and I stare at it. The girl in the photo has dark hair and eyes; she looks nothing like my sister. It says she's twenty-three.

"They don't really care, as long as you have something," she explains. "How's Mary?"

"I don't know. Alright I guess. We don't hang out much anymore." Mary was my best friend during seventh and eighth grade. We spent every minute together, but our friendship did not survive the transition to high school. We have different lunch periods, we are in different tracks, and worst of all, Mary has gone and grown actual breasts over the summer, an act that felt like an unbearable betrayal, even if she had no control over it.

We are both quiet for a moment and I shift around nervously. "Look at my feet!" I say, pointing. "Why couldn't big boobs run in our family?"

She laughs and rolls her eyes. "Hey, do you wanna come out tonight? We're going to the Mann to hear Steve Miller Band. We're just gonna hang outside."

"Oh, okay," I say, trying to play cool.

It's a warm fall night and the lot is packed when we get there. My sister's friend Damon hands me a beer and we begin walking around, checking out the scene. The music is faint but audible. We can make out the roar of the crowd at the end of each song. Kids stand around at the back of cars, pulling beers from coolers. I toss my can and Damon pulls another from his pocket. A police officer on horseback trots right by me without so much as a glance.

I'm just about done with my second beer when I see some of the senior girls from the soccer team. Carolyn Amoroso, who everyone calls "Ammo," is standing next to Eileen Kiefer. They are thin and pretty and surrounded by a slew of popular boys who are jockeying for their attention.

"AMMO! KIEFER!" I scream. I've never spoken directly to either of them, but I begin waving my arm wildly above my head. They turn in my direction with startled expressions. When they see me they look confused. They hold up their hands in half-hearted waves. My arm is still flapping around when my sister grabs me by the neck and pulls me in the opposite direction.

"How many beers have you had?"

"Two," I say proudly, holding up my near-empty can.

"Oh God, you're drunk. No more beer."

Night on the Town

THE TWO SISTERS go to a bar together. Not the one right by their apartment where they've been going since Dani graduated from college a few months ago. This time it's the trendy new Mexican place.

Alexis flags the bartender down with a practiced wave. "I'll have a glass of Cabernet," she says. "What do you want?"

"A Corona, I guess," Dani says, eyeing her.

Alexis knows this outing is a test. Can she stop at just one? Will that be enough? Just last night Dani found her passed out on the bathroom floor, her body blocking the door, making it all but impossible to open. Alexis didn't know how she had wound up there. Had she felt sick? Had she fallen off the toilet? She didn't have any fresh bruises, so that scenario seemed unlikely.

She looks over at her kid sister, who holds her beer in her right hand. The bottle rests loosely between her legs on the barstool. Her back is to the bar and her eyes are focused on the singer who strums his guitar. The fingers on her left hand tap her leg in time with the music.

"Did you hear Gilbert today?" Alexis asks.

"I think everyone heard Gilbert today," Dani says, smirking.

"He's such a goon."

"Oh c'mon, you love bantering with him."

"Sometimes. But sometimes I'm busy trying to make deadline and he can't take a hint," she says.

Gilbert works at the newspaper where Alexis is a reporter. He visits her desk nearly every day and announces his opinion on recent movie releases as if he's proclaiming the gospel. He loves trashing Leonardo DiCaprio's films because he knows that she adores him.

Thanks to her, Dani also works at the paper as an intern. After graduating from Loyola, Alexis invited her kid sister to move into her two-bedroom apartment in one of Baltimore's trendy neighborhoods. Dani spent the summer waitressing at a restaurant in Fells Point. Each night when the restaurant closed, the staff would head up to a favorite bar called Friends, which Alexis frequented. Often when Dani came through the doors at 11, Alexis was already in the back room playing pool and smoking cigarettes. After the summer, when the crowds and the tips started to dry up, Alexis offered to find out about the possibility of a paid internship.

Some days they take the bus together to save money on parking, but other days—even when Dani pounds on her door, or comes in and sits on her bed and tenderly strokes her hair, or yells at her to please get up—Alexis can't bring herself to get out of bed. And finally, Dani will give up and leave without her.

Earlier today, when they got home from work, Dani looked worried and said that they needed to talk, so they sat together in their T.V. room just off the kitchen. "Your drinking is scaring me," Dani told her. "I found a cigarette burned into the rug the other morning. You could've started a fire, for God's sake. Not to mention all the work you've been missing."

Alexis was quiet, wondering when they'd reversed roles. She could feel her younger sister's large blue eyes boring into her, scanning, searching. Her eyes had always been that way—hungry for something—but they used to be softer. They used to study her in order to memorize, in order to replicate what they saw. Lately it feels like the exact opposite.

She knew better than to argue with what her sister was saying about her drinking. Denial was an obvious red flag.

"I'm sorry, Dani," she said. "You're right. I'll take it down a level. I've been really stressed."

"You're more than stressed. You're depressed too, and I want to help, but I don't know if I'm helping or hurting by waking you up every morning. So from now on, if you're drinking the night before, I'm not going to wake you up for work. Like, I'm not even going to knock on your door."

"That's fine. I understand completely. Look, let's go out after dinner for a drink. Just one. You'll see. I heard that Austin Grille has live music."

And so they have wound up here. A chance for her to show her younger sister that everything is fine. The bartender places the glass of wine on a paper coaster. She hopes it will help erase the tension that accumulated in her shoulders while she sat hunched over her computer trying to make deadline on another story at work.

The first sip lights up her taste buds. She recalls a diagram of the tongue that she learned in the fourth grade. Sweet, bitter, salty, sour; imagines taste buds popping up like the figures in a whack-a-mole game. Swelling, then shrinking. The aftertaste of the wine lingers—it reminds her of the sand after the tide recedes, the way that the moisture is sucked up but remains just beneath the surface.

The warmth slides down into her. She thinks of alcohol like oxygen blown on smoldering embers, a thing that can cause flames to erupt. One minute a glowing speck, the next a fiery blaze. Nothing, and then something. It's this potential that she is most drawn to, not the oblivion, though eventually that comes. When she drinks, she feels herself open up, a flower turning toward the sun. In its absence she is closed, her colors and beauty folded in upon themselves.

Lately there's been a palpable tension between herself and Dani, but last week there was the briefest respite when Dani confessed, tearfully, that she thought she might be gay. Upon hearing this, she wrapped her little sister up in her arms and said, "That's great," which only made Dani cry more.

Their hug lasted several minutes. When she let go, Dani looked at her in the quiet, studious way that was fueled by admiration. It had been so long since she'd been looked at this way, and she felt, at that moment, like the world wasn't such a dark place, like maybe things would be okay. She resolved to cut back on her drinking; to make a list of goals; to stop sleeping so much; to stop missing so much work.

On her barstool, Dani bops along to the music and taps her foot. She looks just like their mother: fair-skinned with a long, pointy nose and denim blue eyes. She was a late bloomer and she cannot see anything beautiful about her physical self. She's grown more self-assured over the past couple of years, but she's still woefully insecure, with shadows of desperation similar to those of a hooked fish flopping erratically on the deck of a boat. It pains Alexis to see her sister struggle this way, but she knows the struggles are what will make her strong, so she forces herself to stand back and bear witness. She whispers prayers that her sister will find her way back to the water so she can breathe.

"What?" Dani says when she notices that she's being watched.

"Nothing, it's just that you look a lot like Mom."

"Ugh, my nose?"

"No! I wish you could see yourself. You're pretty."

"Please. You've always been the beautiful one."

Hearing this thrills her, though she doesn't believe it for a second. She sips her wine. She wants another, but she knows better; knows that her recent behavior has been troubling. In truth, she couldn't remember a time when she'd been what anyone would call "normal." When she was a teenager she drew lines across her wrist with dull razors, then covered them with long sleeve shirts. How could she explain the relief that the pain brought with it? This discovery had been nothing short of a miracle for her teenage self. For her, being alive had always felt like being wrapped in gauze until that first time she'd run a blade over her skin. It was in that moment that she first felt like she could breathe, like she'd found a way to survive in the world.

"Are you ready to go?" Dani asks. "We have to be up early for work."

In the bar, people are clapping for the singer, who is going on break. He unplugs his guitar, places it into the stand, then disappears in the direction of the restrooms. Her sister's eyes scan everything, flit to her now-empty wine glass, and then back to her face.

She isn't ready, but she nods, throws a couple of ones on the bar before getting up. There's an open bottle of white wine on the fridge door. She'll have a glass, one glass, she promises herself, then she'll go to bed.

The next morning her alarm blares loud music and she tries to get out of bed, but her body is so heavy. She hears the door to the apartment slam shut. As promised, Dani did not bang on her door, did not tell her to wake up or that it was time for work, or that she was leaving for the bus. She turns off her alarm and absolute quiet descends—the beautiful, horrid silence of being alone.

Morning After Austin Grille

As I pour milk over my cereal, I strain to hear if Alexis is stirring, but there's nothing other than the blaring music from her radio alarm clock. Each creak and groan from the pipes in our apartment sends a false ripple of hope through my body that maybe she's awake. Every part of me wants to go in her room and shake her, force her out of bed, but just last night I told her that I'd no longer wake her if she'd been drinking the night before, and something inside of me knows that I need to stick to this rule.

Lately, I spend large chunks of each day debating whether my sister has a drinking problem or whether she is depressed. This feels very much like an either-or situation: either she is drinking too much because she is depressed, or she is an alcoholic and that is making her depressed. I turn this over and over as if it's a complex riddle that I can solve with enough steely determination; as if the answer will provide a roadmap of what to do or how to act. If it's the former, tenderness and encouragement are required, whereas the latter demands tough love, so as not to enable her.

I sit down at our table, a hand-me-down from our parents, which is jammed into the corner of our tiny kitchen. It's a white laminate top in the shape of a circle that has four 70s mod metal chairs. Growing up, Alexis and I sat across from one another at this table every night, making faces and giggling or complaining that the roast beef was too fatty. Now we rarely sit here. Mostly, the table has become a catchall for mail and other random junk, but this morning I want to be as far from the blaring music as possible.

I fiddle with the button on my shirt and look at my watch. Five minutes until I have to leave. From her room I hear the radio announcer's raucous, throaty laugh. His sidekick, a woman, scolds him when he says outrageous things and he laughs in response. I put my bowl in the sink and return the milk to the fridge. The bottle of white wine on the side door is still half full, which means that she really didn't drink that much last night. Maybe I should at least call her once to tell her I'm leaving. I stand with the refrigerator door open, staring at the wine.

Suddenly, I grab the bottle, uncork it, hold it under my nose, and inhale deeply. I smell nothing. Then, as if my body is moving without my permission, as if it is telling my brain what to do, I'm pouring liquid from the bottle into a glass and drinking it.

It's water.

The strangest feeling comes over me as I process the fact that Alexis filled the bottle with water to make it look like she hadn't drunk the remainder. It's a feeling of yes and no. Of *I KNEW it!* and *What now?* Of validation and panic and deep despair. I let out a long breath. I'm not crazy. This is a real problem.

I've had moments of clarity like this before, where I've understood that Alexis is in trouble, but denial has always acted like quicksand, making them disappear before I could process them, but this time feels different. Denial sits quietly on the sidelines, as if it knows better than to try to smokescreen this one. A weight settles on my chest.

She needs help.

I place the bottle back on the side rack, so she won't know that I know. For some reason, it feels important to keep this knowledge in my back pocket. I grab my bag, walk quietly down the steps, and then slam the door with every ounce of energy in my body.

A Spot in the Earth

"Ask for John," Brigid tells us when we leave the funeral home to head over to the cemetery, "he'll take care of you." In my hand, I carry a pad of paper where I've been writing down the list of things that need to be done. It has grown exponentially since we walked into Riley's. There are pictures to be emailed for the obituary and mass card, text to be chosen for the card, a quote for the obituary, and a woman to be contacted about making a program for the mass.

At the cemetery office, we are informed that John is out with other clients and we will have to wait. A man with a magnificent comb-over of dyed red hair steps out of a room. He wears an ill-fitting navy suit with a pink plaid tie.

"I'm happy to help you folks," he says. "I'm Herb." The three of us look at one another, trying to decide if we are going to wait or settle for Herb.

My mother reaches for her watch. "It's already past three."

With that my father steps forward and shakes his hand. Herb it is.

"Shall we?" Herb points toward a room.

He holds the door as we file in. The room has a round table and glaring fluorescent lights. As soon as we sit, he dives right in.

"If you want a headstone, the smallest lot that you can purchase has six plots. The sites with the flat stone markers only hold two plots. These days, six plots means six burials regardless of whether that's a coffin or an urn. Years ago, you could bury two coffins and two urns on a two-plot site, but not anymore. The rules have changed."

I hate the way he talks so easily of all of this, as if we're discussing possible paint colors for the walls of a house.

He stands up and grabs some papers, taps them on the table to straighten them, and then passes the pile to us. Herb's cologne has filled the room. The smell reminds me of sharp corners and clean edges.

"All over the cemetery," he says, waving his arms, "there are lots that are the same size, but each one has different rules depending on what year it was purchased."

What a goddamn scam, I think. On top of the stack of papers is a map of the cemetery. Herb circles areas where there are available lots.

"I can bring you to these areas so you can see them," he offers with a sudden gentleness that surprises me.

We climb into Herb's car. In the backseat there's a box of tissues between my mom and me. *Maybe he's not so bad*, I think as I grab a tissue and blow my nose into it.

Herb drives slowly around the curvy roads of St. Peter and Paul. I smile as I recall that the first time I ever got drunk, I was with Alexis in a cemetery. She brought me there to hang out with her friends, who all called it "the cem."

There are no lots available near where my mother's parents are buried, nor any in the section that houses my father's family. My father's Aunt Phyllis has offered a spot for Alexis in the plot that she owns, but my mother has declined.

"I want her with us," she'd said to my father when he'd mentioned this offer, which sent a shockwave of jealousy right down the center of me. With us. *What about me*, I'd wanted to scream, despite the fact that I had no desire to be buried, and even if I did have such a desire, I'd be buried next to my wife who, it just so happened, also did not want to be buried. Still, when I heard my mother say this, *I want her with us*, my mind flashed to the future, to a day when I would stand over the grave of all three of them—Mother, Father, Sister, lying next to one another for eternity, and in this flash forward, I felt a loneliness deeper than ever before.

Herb pulls the car over in the front section of the cemetery, near the busy road by the main entrance. He explains the numbering system for the plots, and points to engraved numbers on the side of each headstone that are connected to the system. I nod my head without understanding and look around at all the graves. There are so many dead people. Some of the stones have names with no dates filled in and I quickly surmise that these are plots that have been purchased by people who are still living. Planners. Could there be anything more depressing than buying your own burial plot? But on the flip side, it spares your family members from having to do it, as we are now.

When we get back in the car to drive to the other section, I begin to cry, quietly at first, trying to keep it to myself, but it builds into heaving sobs. My mother begins too and we pull tissues out of the box and hand them to one another.

Herb rattles on in the front, either unaware or uninterested in the breakdowns occurring in the backseat. Or maybe he thinks his aimless talk is the best way to cover up our sobs and therefore give us space to cry. "Hoo boy," he says, "at five o'clock when the gates lock around here, it's like a dinner whistle for the deer. They come out and eat all the flowers on the graves."

My grandfather once told Alexis and me about how he put razor blades in the roses on my grandma's grave because he'd gotten tired of the deer eating them. My sister and I had both looked at one another with our jaws dropped open and our eyes wide. "Pop," she'd cried, "those poor deer. That's awful." He'd just chuckled.

"Now," Herb says as he pulls the car over again, "this is a much quieter section."

"What's back there?" my father asks, pointing to an area a few hundred yards from the road where a big line of trees stands, just before the earth slopes down.

"It's some kind of retention pond or something," Herb says.

"Well I don't want a spot back by anything swampy," my father says, as if Herb is trying to swindle us. "Are any of these lots available?" He points to an area under a tree.

Herb consults his diagram and motions to a few nearby.

"I think she'd like to be under a tree," my father says to no one in particular. His soft voice hangs in the air. Everybody is quiet as we stand there, even Herb. Something about this place feels right and I know this will be her spot in the earth, and that one day it'll be my mother and father's spot too.

Boobies

I CALL TO Alexis from the bottom of the stairs that lead to her attic bedroom. "Lex?"

"Hang on a sec," I hear her say into the telephone. "What?"

"Can I come up?" I ask, my voice hesitant, wavering a bit. "I need to talk to you."

"Hey Jason, I'm gonna have to call you back, my sister wants something. I love you too." I hear the phone being placed into its cradle. "C'mon up!"

I let out a breath, feeling both relieved and guilty that Alexis has ended her phone call with her boyfriend on my behalf. A couple of years ago, our parents let Alexis move her bedroom from the second floor to the attic so she could have more privacy. They'd gotten it carpeted and had the tiny bathroom redone. Alexis loves it up here, even though it gets really hot in the summer. She says it's like her own apartment where she can play her music loud and sneak cigarettes late at night when everyone else is sleeping. A poster of Sid Vicious, the bassist from the Sex Pistols, hangs on the wall. She aspires to his attitude of not giving a fuck.

"Hi," I say sheepishly, standing in the doorway. "Sorry if I interrupted."

"It's okay. Colleen will be here any minute anyway. I think we're going to make some Ellio's pizza and play Tetris."

"Oh, cool," I say, fidgeting with my hands, lacing them together, then unlacing them.

"Come in," Alexis says softly. "What's up?"

I sigh. The last time I'd stood here like this it was because I'd gotten in a fight with my best friend, Mary, and we hadn't spoken for an entire day, not even at school, and I didn't know what to do.

Being able to confide in Alexis is a relatively new phenomenon. Just a couple of years ago our relationship had been one of pure antagonism with me constantly snooping in her room and reading her diaries, but something shifted in the last year, and ever since, I've begun showing up in her room more and more. Alexis never sends me away when she senses that I'm upset, even if I've pissed her off by stealing one of her CDs or borrowing a shirt without asking.

All at once I flop onto the bed and start crying. Alexis wraps her arms around me and waits a beat. "What's going on?"

"I think I have breast cancer," I blurt.

"Dani, why do you think that?" she asks, managing to keep a straight face.

"Because I have a lump, right here." I point to my left breast. My eyes are wet with tears and I can barely allow them to meet Lex's before looking away, embarrassed.

"Can you show me?"

I hesitate, then grab Lex's hand and place it on the lump, right beneath my nipple. "It's right here. It feels different from the other boob."

I watch Alexis's face as she moves her fingers around the small, hard mass that I discovered earlier. On my favorite show, *Beverly Hills 90210*, Brenda found a lump in her breast after getting hit by a volleyball, and she had to get something called a biopsy.

After what feels like an eternity, Alexis draws her hand back and smiles.

"What are you smiling about?" I ask angrily.

"Dani, that's not cancer. It's just your boob starting to grow."

"My boob? That's my boob?"

"That's your boob!"

"That's my boob! Finally! My boob! Woooo. Wait, where's my other boob?"

"I'm sure it's coming," Alexis says, laughing as she wraps one arm around my neck and messes my hair up with the other. "You're such a goober."

"Hello?" a voice calls from the kitchen.

We both jump at the sound. "Colleen's here!" Lex says. "C'mon." She grabs my hand and we rush down to the kitchen.

"Coooooolllllleeeeeen," Lex calls as we run. "Guess what?"

Alexis and I slide onto the kitchen tile with our socked feet.

"I'm growing boobies!" I shout before Lex can spill the news. I throw my arms above my head triumphantly.

"She's growing boobies!" Lex yells elatedly.

"You're growing boobies? Hooray for you!" Colleen says.

The three of us keel over laughing.

"C'mon," Lex says, grabbing our hands and pulling us outside to the back patio where the three of us climb up onto the picnic table that our dad built. We join hands and jump up and down as Lex sings: "You're getting boobies, you're getting boobies. You no have cancer, you just grow boobies!"

Colleen and I join in between fits of laughter, tears streaming down our faces.

Not Always a Note

Several months after Alexis's death, I get an email from a friend who lost two of her brothers to suicide by hanging.

I'm so glad that your sister left you a note—from talking with my brothers and my depressed lover I know that must have taken a huge effort on your sister's part, just to separate from the pain and think of you all.

Gratitude courses through me when I read her words, along with a great ache for my sister. In the past, Alexis's suicide notes elicited only anger from me, but this time is different. Perhaps because I feel absolved by the words, "Tell Dani I love her."

A vision of Alexis comes to me. In it, she stands at the counter, scribbling her note on the Post-it pad, weeping.

I yearn to be with her in that moment, to tell her not to worry about us, to go rest, that she deserves some peace. I wish I could whisper in her ear, the way that people do to dying relatives in hospice, that it's okay to let go; that I understand her choice; that I don't want her to suffer one minute longer.

Even years later, this desire will remain. The thing that makes me saddest about her death is that she had to go through it alone.

NAMI

IT'S 2013 WHEN I enroll in a class through the National Alliance for the Mentally Ill (NAMI) for family members of those who have a "loved one" who is mentally ill. I sign up after Alexis has a seizure one night and doesn't regain consciousness for a full week, during which time I am convinced that she will die and plagued with guilt that I could have done more to love her.

In the class, we learn to say, "my loved one who has a mental illness," instead of "my mentally ill loved one," because the emphasis should be on the person, not the disease. We learn about all the different types of mental illness and about the medications used to treat each type. We do exercises intended to help us build empathy and understanding. In one exercise we break into small groups. One person attempts to perform a task while the other members of the group stand behind us calling things out to us, so we can understand what it might feel like to have an auditory hallucination.

Over the weeks of the course, we get to know each other and learn about each person's loved one. Most of the class consists of parents and spouses, but there is one other woman who has a sister with mental illness. Despite her presence, I feel out of place in the group because I am so far removed from my sister's daily care.

Nobody at NAMI talks about being angry so I don't talk about it either, but I am. I am a pot boiled over, I am teeth grinding together, I am the screech of brakes just before an accident. I am angry at the person my sister has become and the toll it has taken on my parents. I am most comfortable with my anger when it exists on behalf of others. Here, in this class, we are supposed to be empathic caregivers. Here, I call my sister a "loved one." I don't mention that I struggle to love my loved one.

There are two individuals who lead the class—one man, one woman—both of whom have children who are mentally ill. The woman says that when you tell a person who has mental illness to try harder, it's the same as telling a nearsighted person to try to see something in the distance without the aid of glasses. I think of all the times I have thought about the fact that my sister doesn't seem to want to get better, the way that I have blamed her for her illness. I ache with regret, but if I did not feel angry with her, I would be left with only the deepest despair. Anger is so much safer.

One thing I learn in the class is that the dynamics that tend to crop up between parents and their loved ones are different from the ones that typically develop among siblings with a loved one who is ill. Parents will stop at nothing to help their child. They'll sacrifice their lives for a slim chance at normalcy. They tend to feel responsible.

Siblings typically harbor very different emotions. There is often more of a need and ability to separate from the loved one. One mother in the group talks to me about the way that her kids have responded to their sibling's illness. They are angry, resentful, tired of the constant attention poured onto the sick child. This feels both accurate and not quite right. I've become comfortable with a certain level of invisibility in my family. It has allowed me a freedom that wouldn't exist otherwise. My parents lack the energy required to closely scrutinize my life. Also, even though I've chosen a low-paying career as a writer and cabinetmaker, I'm still held out as the successful one. As long as I am not sick, I am better off than my sister who can no longer hold down a job. When it comes to my relationship with my parents, I feel both wonderfully independent and utterly abandoned.

The Story

THE STORY THAT I tell myself about Alexis's death is that she took the overdose of pills some hours after midnight on Saturday, around 3 or 4 a.m.

My mom called some hours later. I don't know what time because I forget to make note of it when she first tells me, and later when I wonder, I don't want to make her recount the details, but whatever time it was, Alexis answered the phone, sounding garbled and groggy.

"Oh, I didn't mean to wake you. Go back to sleep," my mom had said.

Go back to sleep.

"Make sure you put the phone on the charger."

This must be the reason that my sister's body was on the floor when she was found. She got out of bed to return the phone to the cradle, and she fell. I can't bear to think that Alexis might've gotten out of bed because she changed her mind.

But I keep wondering whether she got scared as she lay dying, whether she thought it was a mistake to have taken all those pills.

In her memoir, *An Unquiet Mind*, Kay Redfield Jamison recounts how, during her own attempted overdose, her brother called her. Somehow, in the haze of unconsciousness, her body reacted to the phone ringing and she answered it. The moment her brother heard her speak, he knew something wasn't right and he called for paramedics to be dispatched to her home.

What if Alexis had been saved? What if *I* had called her just to say *hello, I love you*? What if?

The only answer I can allow myself to believe is that she would have suffered another couple of months or years before she tried to kill herself again.

I tell myself that there wouldn't have been any happiness greater than her pain.

I tell myself that she is better off dead than suffering.

I tell myself not to think of the beautiful sunsets she might have seen; the small joys that might have warmed her soul—a crescent moon hanging in the night sky, as she so loved, or the feel of her feet in the sand.

This is the story I tell myself and tell myself and tell myself.

It doesn't matter whether it's true. It only matters that I believe it. Truth does not need to hold hands with belief.

Sign Here

WHEN WE GET back to the office from our tour of the cemetery with Herb, we sit at a table under the glare of the harsh fluorescent light while we wait for paperwork to be gathered. Outside, the sun is still bright and warm, though it's nearly five o'clock. I wonder whether Alexis would be sad about missing such a beautiful spring day, whether a day like this might've made her want to keep on living. I'll have this thought constantly in the first months whenever I see something beautiful.

Herb returns with a stack of papers. The way his hair is cut around his slightly pointy ears reminds me of an elf. I wonder how long he's been in this business. He seems much better suited to sell things that people would be happy to buy, like a car or a new pair of shoes. I imagine him in another setting with a whole script of corny jokes and pleasantries that aren't appropriate in this setting; imagine him going through some sort of training for this job and his supervisor shaking his head somberly each time Herb got too chummy with the customer.

Herb points to the sheet that has all of the line items and their cost. In addition to the lot, there's a burial fee, a fee for a foundation that the headstone rests on, and an administrator's fee.

"Also, do you think you'll need a tent for the funeral?" he asks. "A tent is extra."

"I don't know," my father says, looking to my mother, "what do you think?"

I glance at my phone to check the weather forecast. "Looks like it's going to be nice, but it might be hot."

Just then my father's phone rings. "It's the medical examiner," he says.

"Can you give us a minute alone?" my mother asks Herb. He nods and steps out of the room.

"Hello?" my father says into his phone. He waves his arm at my mother for a pen and she fishes in her purse and hands it to him. He begins to scribble things down. My mother and I lean in to see what he's writing.

Large qty. small white pills.

Herb pops back in. I shake my head no. The sound of the pen scratching out my father's pointy writing fills the room.

XR 300

"What about a time of death?" My father's voice is steady, his brow creased in concentration as he listens.

Herb cracks open the door, sees my father still on the phone, and closes it again.

"When will you have the full results?"

My mother massages her temples. I reach over and rub her back.

When my father hangs up, he looks down at the paper.

"He said she had a lot of small white pills in her stomach and that there were also capsules that said XR 300. Four to six weeks before the final results are in. They'll call us."

"Six weeks? That long?" my mother says.

I type "XR 300" into my phone. Seroquel. One of Alexis's many prescriptions. I read quickly, trying to make sense of how we have come to be sitting in this office the day after my parents' 46th wedding anniversary, but all I learn is that Seroquel is an atypical antipsychotic that is commonly used to treat Bipolar and Major Depressive Disorder.

The door opens again and Herb sees that my father is off the phone. He steps in and waits a beat before asking, "What'd we decide about the tent?"

I look up from my screen, amazed by his tactlessness.

"We should probably just get one," my mother says to no one in particular.

Herb disappears for a moment and reemerges with one more piece of paper that he adds to the stack in front of my father. My father sits hunched, studying the documents while Herb hovers over his shoulder pointing to where he needs to sign.

"Is there some kind of payment plan?" my dad asks.

"Oh no," Herb says. "I'll need the full balance today."

My father's brows rise and his mouth opens as if he's going to argue, then he sighs and opens his checkbook in resignation. He tears a check off and hands it to Herb before we leave.

"God, what a creep," I say when we get back into our car to leave. "Herb. Who names their kid Herb?"

We all burst out laughing, which feels both odd and completely necessary. This day has pumped me full of tension. Every time I jotted a note down on my pad of paper, every time I added something to the list of things to do, I felt more and more stretched. All day I've been scouring my brain, trying to imagine what Alexis would want. I keep feeling waves of panic that we are getting it all wrong. This funeral will be her last hurrah, and I know that she'd want it to be a grand affair, that she'd want everything just so. I can almost feel her looking down on us, grading us on our performance, shaking her head in disappointment. We keep joking around that she'll haunt us if we make the wrong decisions, but I am at least partly serious. When we all laugh about Herb, I feel like a balloon losing air, flying around the room in a burst of glee, before falling flat on the ground.

"Oh man, that guy was slick," my dad says.

"I'm glad we picked that spot in the quieter section," I say. "I think that Alexis will like it better there than the one by the road." *Will like*, I think, noting that I'm talking about her in a future tense. As if she is still an entity that can like or dislike things. I suddenly recall the many conversations I had with my mother when Alexis was alive, things I said: *I hope she will decide that she wants to get better*.

Will decide. As if it were that simple.

"Look!" I yell, pointing to a spot in the grass where a tiny fawn has curled itself into a ball. My father slows the car to a crawl and we all stare. The fawn's legs are tucked tightly underneath its body and its ears are pinned back in fear. An overwhelming urge to protect this creature surges inside of me. I think of what Herb said about the deer coming out at dusk and then of my grandfather and the way that he hid razor blades inside of roses he left on my grandmother's grave.

Generosity

My mother has doubts about how Alexis died and it bothers me more than it should, but I can't nail down the reason that it upsets me so much.

"My therapist isn't convinced that Alexis killed herself either, even with the note that she left," my mom tells me one day on the phone several weeks after Alexis's death. "She thinks that Alexis had a few drinks and took a few pills and just didn't wake up."

"Hmmm," I say, but inside I am fuming at the therapist's implied nonchalance that Alexis supposedly took over life or death. At the element of chance. At the idea that she didn't mean to die.

It's true that there are only a handful of undeniable facts surrounding my sister's death: the pills, the alcohol, the note. The rest is all conjecture, a big fat question mark. We will each—my mother, my father, and myself—tell ourselves the story we need to hear in order to get through the day.

My mother's version has Alexis's death as an accident. As proof, my mother circles back to a bunch of appointments that

Alexis scheduled for the day after my parents returned from Florida: to the hairdresser, the eye doctor, the neurologist. My mother had offered to shuttle her around to each of these since she wasn't due back at work until Wednesday.

"Why would she make all of those appointments if she was planning to kill herself?" she asks, her voice thick with confusion.

It's a good question, a fair question—one that I have turned over in my mind, one that I don't have an answer for.

"I don't know, Mom, it doesn't make any sense to me either. But why did she leave that note? Why did she say, 'Tell Dani I love her?' Why would she even mention me?"

"I don't know, but I told my therapist that I'm coming to the conclusion that this was all part of God's plan," my mom says. "That God looked at Alexis and said, 'You've suffered enough, child' and then took her from this earth into His arms."

I search for something in my mom's statement that I can agree with, trying to understand her and what she needs to believe. Yes, Alexis had suffered enough, but God's plan? I cannot get behind that. Fuck that. *Fuck God's plan*, I think.

"What Alexis lived through," my mom continues. "She's my hero."

I push down the thing that I want to scream: *What about me*? The question moves through me like boiling water, not still enough to pin down, partly evaporating when it reaches the surface. I feel like a bitter, jealous child. I tell myself that I don't know the first thing about suffering; that I have a nice life, a functioning brain. I have the world. I should be grateful, not jealous, but the word *hero* is like acid eating through the veneer of the graciousness that I usually present to the world.

These words will stick with me. *Alexis is my hero*. I will replay them in my head, and each time I will feel so angry.

In the coming months, my mother and I will have different versions of this same conversation. For a while, I argue with my mother by offering counterpoints every time she cites a piece of evidence that might support her belief.

Eventually I stop because it dawns on me that my mother needs her story as much as I need mine. I come to understand that she cannot believe that her daughter chose to die because that might mean something awful about the way she loved Alexis. I learn that keeping my mouth shut is a generosity that I can easily give.

Psychic

My mother was the last person to speak to my sister before she died. She goes over and over the last words in her mind.

"Did I say I love you when we were getting off the phone?" she asks my father. He says he thinks so.

"I just wish I could remember whether I told her that I loved her," she says to me.

"She knew, Mom. Even if you didn't say it, she knew," I tell her.

She goes to see a psychic. "Yes," he tells her when she asks, "of course you told her."

After that, she doesn't ask anymore.

The Outfit

When my parents and I arrive back at their house after our long day of meeting with the priest, the undertaker, and of course Herb, there are packages on the steps: several floral arrangements and a white paper bag filled with four heavy-duty foil containers—chicken parmesan, baked ziti, and two different kinds of lasagna. Later, an Edible Arrangement arrives along with a tray of hoagies cut into bite-sized pieces.

We quickly run out of places to put the flowers and I find my body stiffening whenever the doorbell rings with another delivery. Part of me is grateful, but what the hell are we supposed to do with twenty floral arrangements? One moment I find the orchid plant sent by one of Lindsay's sisters beautiful, the next minute I want to throw it in the garbage.

Later that evening my mother and I go through Alexis's overstuffed closet to look for an outfit for her cremation. Earlier at the funeral home, Brigid mentioned that this was a thing we could do, and much to my surprise, I felt a wash of relief when she said it. I'd always found it odd whenever

I heard about people choosing clothes for a dead person to be buried in, and now, suddenly I understand perfectly. It seems like a thing that would matter to Alexis, so it matters to me. Maybe it's a chance to erase the image of her body on the floor.

"How about this?" I ask my mother, pulling out a black satin top that Alexis wore to the Philadelphia flower show, a detail I know only because there was a photo of her taken on that day where she stood in front of a stunning montage of flowers, looking small and shy and happy.

"Maybe," my mother says without conviction.

As we search, my mother's eye catches on a red sequined dress that Alexis wore to our cousin's wedding.

"That's it," my mother says definitively. "She looked like a million bucks that night. We need to find the red shoes."

There's a photo from that night that shows Alexis, my mother, and me on the dance floor. My mother's mouth is open in what looks like a happy shout and my sister leans into the two of us with her arms spread out in a "ta-da" stance. I stand behind them with my arms raised above my head. We are a rainbow of colors—bright green on my mom, blue on me, and sparkling red sequins on Alexis.

That photo of us out on the dance floor caught us in a rare moment of lightness, but for the majority of the reception I'd been braced with worry that Alexis would do or say something inappropriate. And indeed, by the end of the night she'd gotten so drunk that she fell over as we walked toward the elevators.

Thinking of that photo now as I dig through the boxes of shoes on the floor of the closet, it feels like my memories are being run through the filter of loss. Things that had infuriated me less than forty-eight hours ago are fast becoming stories that I find myself telling with a wistful laugh.

The image captured that evening was the exception, not

the rule, yet I can feel this happy image pushing all the others out of its way, sliding through the filter and leaving behind the moments where I struggled to be nice to my sister, where I felt embarrassed by the way she sidled up to some guy on the dance floor.

If I wanted, I could simply look at the photo where we all appear so happy, so much like a family, and I could reduce that night to one uncomplicated sentence. Something like, "That was such a good time." I could pretend that this sentence was the whole truth. Was that what I should be doing? Was that the kind thing to do?

I pull a shoebox out from the bottom of a stack and open it to find a pair of red patent leather pumps.

"Yup, those are the ones," my mother says. I feel reassured by the certainty in her voice.

My mother puts the dress and shoes that we have chosen for Alexis's cremation into a box with tissue paper, the way that she'd do when wrapping a present.

Drive

LATER THAT NIGHT, my father, mother, and I sit at the kitchen table eating one of the lasagnas that was sent to the house. The pasta is homemade and deliciously soft. It feels strange to actually enjoy eating a meal.

"I should've bought her a car," my mother says suddenly. Her face turns bright red and the fork in her hand trembles.

Alexis hadn't driven a car in at least five years. Not since she'd wrecked the Pontiac Bonneville that my father had sold to her. After that, my parents wouldn't allow her to borrow their cars and she couldn't afford one of her own, so not driving was just a thing that sort of happened. A thing that I'd always thought of as a blessing—one less worry for everybody. I'd assumed that my mother and father felt the same, so I'm jolted to hear my mom express regret over this.

I know that my mother is tightly weaving a story in her mind, a story in which something she did or did not do led to Alexis's death. I want to point out all of the ways that buying Alexis a car would've been a disaster, as if this might somehow loosen the knots of blame that my mother's brain is tying, but I say nothing. I simply swirl pasta around my plate, tallying my own list of illogical regrets, small, inconsequential things—a phone call, a hug, a card—and wondering whether they could have made a difference.

Echoes

I'M SITTING AT Lindsay's parents' house for a family gathering several months after Alexis's death. My sister-in-law, the chatty one, is talking about some function that she attended with her family at church. Her long, dark hair flows around her face. I look at her without really seeing her. I'm grateful that there are other people in the room to listen to her story because I feel like I am underwater.

This is the way that conversations come through to me now. I hear words, but they are muddled and far away, as if whoever is talking is on another floor of a house. I do my best to pretend, but things that used to feel normal now strike me as so odd, like the way people talk with such fervor about how someone cut them off in traffic. *Who cares*, I think.

Each day when I walk into my life, it feels like I am entering my home after being away on a long trip. I look around and see the blanket that I left crumpled on the couch, but for the life of me I don't remember being the one who sat there nestled in that blanket. Everything is the same, but also completely unrecognizable in this way I can't name.

A Cold Fear

As I DRIVE home from the cabinet shop one day in late October, my friend Meg's name pops up on the caller ID screen in my car. Meg was the friend I'd been helping on the day that my sister called after she'd turned the gas on in her apartment. Once upon a time, Meg and I talked every day and confided in one another about everything, but after she'd had her first kid, we'd drifted slowly apart. In the nearly five months that have passed since Alexis's death, Meg and I have barely spoken, so I'm slightly surprised to see she's calling.

"Hello?"

"Rachel and I are splitting up," she blurts.

"Wait, what?" I ask. Meg and Rachel have two kids together. When the distance had crept into our friendship, I'd initially chalked it up to her being busy as a new mom and figured that the relationship between us was in a temporary waning phase, but the less frequently we talked, the more I started to notice how one-sided the conversations were when we did speak. Meg would go on and on about all the happenings in her life and then in what felt like an afterthought, she'd say,

"How are you?" Once I'd noticed this pattern, I found myself less willing to open up to her, which had created a further rift. Meg had attended Alexis's funeral, but other than showing up there and a few sporadic phone calls to check in, she'd been largely absent in my life in a way that would have once been unthinkable in the wake of the death of a loved one. We'd grown so far apart that I hadn't even told Meg that Lindsay and I had started the process of trying to get pregnant.

"I've been having an affair, with Carly from Crossfit," she says.

Something in me recoils at this news, the way a hand does when burned—a kind of reflexive snapping back, suddenly and indelicately. *She's been having,* I think, my brain breaking down the tense. Present-perfect continuous. Still happening.

This didn't compute. Meg brought Rachel coffee in bed every morning and the two of them were always tenderly touching each other at parties, which had always elicited a raw jealousy in me because a part of me wished Lindsay and I were more physically demonstrative. I knew that no relationship was perfect, but they'd always seemed so solidly in love.

"What?" I say again. Carly from Crossfit is married. To a man. With whom she has two kids. I'm having trouble processing the idea that none of these three facts cancel out what I've just been told. My mind jumps to the last conversation I had with Meg when she told me all about how she and Rachel had hosted Carly along with her husband and two girls at their house for homemade brick oven pizza. When had that been? A couple of months ago? Had she already been sleeping with Carly then?

The kids are the thing I keep getting stuck on. Four kids between the two couples. Four kids. My brain swirls this number around and around. Theoretically, I'm not a believer in staying in an unhappy marriage solely for the sake of the kids, but had Meg even tried to stick it out? Besides that, what did it even mean to be happy in a marriage? Experience had taught me that if you were going to be married for a lifetime, you couldn't expect to be happy every moment. Or even every year.

For much of the year prior to Alexis's death, my own marriage had felt both stalled out and hemmed in by a resentment that had been threaded through, what felt to me, like a painstakingly slow journey toward marriage and a family, but Lindsay and I weren't going to split up. Of course we weren't. If I'd learned anything from being married, I'd learned that feelings weren't permanent. Not the ones that felt really good and not the ones that felt really bad. If two people were going to stay together, they had to be willing to work things out *and* wait things out. Lindsay and I were banking on this. Just one day earlier we had gone through our first round of Intrauterine Insemination—a fancy way of saying that a doctor had injected donor sperm into Lindsay's uterus. It's entirely possible that she's pregnant at this very moment or that she's about to be. We would find out in a couple of weeks, when she took a test at the fertility center.

As I drive, I recall that Meg and Rachel had briefly broken up before reconciling, and then very quickly gotten pregnant. I wonder now whether they had merely papered over their problems and whether Lindsay and I might be doing the same with our attempt to get pregnant. A tendril of fear wraps itself around me. Had Lindsay and I just doubled down on our relationship when it would have been wiser to go our separate ways?

"What happened?" I ask, trying to drain the judgment from my tone. I want to say the right thing, but I'm feeling untethered by Meg's declaration. As if her words have cut the anchor line of *my* life and set me adrift on a strong current. If Meg and Rachel were splitting up, no one was safe.

"Rachel and I have really drifted apart since having the boys," she says. "And we both kind of knew it, but whenever I'd bring it up, it got dismissed, like there was never time to deal with it. And then I met Carly and we just clicked. At first, I thought I just really liked this new friend, kind of lying to myself, but then, eventually we both acknowledged that there was more there."

"God," I say to Meg as I put my blinker on to get on the highway. "That's awful. Is there any chance that you'll work through it?"

"No," she says. "I'm a piece of shit, I know, but I'm in love with Carly. I didn't mean for it to happen."

"But, like, why didn't you just tell Rachel?"

"We were going to."

"I mean before you slept together."

"I know. I didn't mean to hurt anyone."

I inhale deeply. This last bit from Meg sounds so cliché and empty, but maybe I'm being too harsh. There's a vulnerability in her words, *I'm a piece of shit*, and I know she's probably desperate to have someone tell her that she's the same person she's always been; that she's still a good person, but all I can muster is, "What do you need? I mean, do you need somewhere to stay?"

This is the least I can do for her. Years ago, when I broke up with my long-term partner, Meg and Rachel had given me the keys to their beach condo and let me live there for free while my partner and I tried to figure out what to do with our house. Meg told me over and over that the two of us had not been right for each other. Meg called me every day and told me to go exercise, to move my body, to not allow myself to sit in despair. In so many ways, it was Meg who had saved me.

"Yeah, maybe. Rachel wants me out of the house."

"Okay, I need to talk to Lindsay. I'm leaving in a day to go to a writing residency for two weeks, so I won't be around."

"Dani," Meg says, "I wanted to tell you sooner."

"Well, I'm glad you didn't," I say harshly. "I would've been pissed if you told me before Rachel." In the silence that follows, I realize how callous this probably sounded. "I mean, I don't think I could handle carrying a secret like that, that's all. Look, I'll talk to Lindsay and I'll text you later."

I drive the rest of the way home in a daze, making a mental spreadsheet of the strengths and weaknesses of my own relationship in order to assess its status. Alexis's death had caused Lindsay and me to draw closer to one another. It cut through the static and haze of routine and allowed us to see one another clearly and to remember that so much of the everyday bullshit wasn't really important. I often thought of the way that Lindsay had been so steady on the day of Alexis's funeral—the way she had ironed the clothes I needed, prompted me to eat when she saw my hands shaking, and curled her body into mine and held me tightly that night. These were acts of love and when I thought of them—and the many others in the months since Alexis's death—they were tangible reminders of how much she cared for me.

But grief had also separated us in a way that surprised me. It was one of the loneliest emotions I'd ever experienced, and while Lindsay could support me in a hundred different ways, she couldn't be in it with me, the same way that I could not be in it with my mother or father, even though we were grieving the loss of the same person. It felt like my life had become a dark tunnel and Lindsay could not walk through that darkness with me. The best she could do was hand me a flashlight to guide me on my journey. The grief was mine and I would either survive it or not, learn to walk with it or surrender to its weight. Despite my best efforts thus far, I didn't feel steady on my feet and I could not yet say with confidence that I was not going to completely unravel in some unhealthy way.

When I arrive home, I recount my conversation with Meg to Lindsay. She's equally shocked, but seems less judgy than my Virgo self.

"What a mess," she says.

"I know," I say. "Is it okay if she stays here for a while?"

"Yeah," Lindsay says without hesitation, which surprises me even though it shouldn't. Generous is Lindsay's default state of being.

That night Meg moves into our guest room and later, the two of us sit in the kitchen talking. I want to be as good of a friend to Meg as she has been to me over the years, but as I sit listening to the details of how everything evolved between her and Carly, I feel myself shifting away from my friend.

"I'm so in love with her," Meg says from where she sits on an island barstool. She pulls a box out of her pocket and waves it in the air. "I got this for Carly, for our two-month anniversary." She opens it, revealing a moon necklace. "We were sitting looking at the moon the first time we kissed." I try to compose my face into an expression that looks interested, but I'm appalled at the way she seems so lovestruck, like a fucking teenager instead of a grown woman with responsibilities. With kids. As she speaks, my brain keeps tracking away from Meg and thinking of Rachel, who's at home with the boys, who must feel so betrayed and hurt.

More than anything, I feel angry with Meg because I think she's giving up too easily. I cling to the anger because it allows me to keep a distance between us, and I'm desperate for the distance. Meg feels dangerous to me. She's fire—burning everything down to follow her heart, and I cannot be around fire.

In the months since Alexis's death, I've been working diligently to control my grief, to keep it contained and small by going to therapy and joining support groups, but I'm afraid of what it might cause me to do to my life if I let it get too big. Maybe I'll self-destruct because I feel guilty for all the ways I failed to love Alexis. Maybe I'll cheat or start drinking too much or just fall apart. None of these things feel out of the realm of possibility and I can't allow myself to be close to a person so willing to surrender the beautiful life she'd built, even if it winds up being for a true and magical love. I need to be surrounded by stability and steadfastness, not by a person willing to yield to rather than fight against. This is the part of me that recoils, the part of me that steps back, rather than drawing close to my longtime friend.

The next morning, when I hear the water running in the pipes from the upstairs bathroom, I rush to finish my cereal before Meg comes down. I don't want to hear any more stories about Carly and how much Meg loves her.

Later that night, I sit on the floor of our bedroom rolling up my T-shirts and stuffing them into a suitcase. Lindsay is in the bathroom standing at the sink. She takes a deep breath and sighs. "Do I really need to brush my teeth *and* wash my face?" This is a question Lindsay speaks out loud whenever she feels extra tired.

"Just pick one and get in bed," I say, laughing.

Tomorrow, I'll drive to a small town in northern Pennsylvania where I'll stay in an old church that's been converted into a home. I'm both excited and terrified about the idea of being alone for two weeks. This residency is where I'm going to begin in earnest writing about my grief, and my fear around this task is palpable, like a metallic taste in one's mouth. But as afraid as I am, I need to go. I kiss the canister of Alexis's ashes that I keep on my windowsill and stuff them into my backpack.

Leaving her ashes behind never crosses my mind. She needs to be with me while I'm away and besides that, I've been meaning to decorate her canister. Earlier in the week, I'd packed a box of Alexis's old art supplies into my car. The box contained at least two binders filled with cutouts she'd chosen from art magazines. I planned to use these to collage the surface of her ash container, the way that she'd done with so many boxes and frames.

Lindsay grabs her toothbrush and begins dutifully scrubbing. "Did you make a list?" she mumbles and nods toward my bag.

"Sort of," I say, motioning to the scribbles I'd started on the back of an envelope.

She pulls the toothbrush out and points it at me. "D! Make a real list."

She's right. I'm a horrible packer, always forgetting some essential item. Once, I'd packed only one dress shoe for a wedding and had to scramble to find shoes at the last minute before the ceremony.

"I'll be fine," I say, zipping my bag closed.

Tomorrow evening I'll be in a strange place, in a strange bed with no T.V. or internet to distract me. Tomorrow, I'll be alone with my grief. Lindsay climbs into bed and I join her, snuggling my body close to hers and thinking of our appointment at the fertility center just two days prior. As I drift to sleep, I wonder how long it takes a sperm to reach an egg. I wonder whether it's possible that this could have already happened inside Lindsay's body. Most of all, I wonder about the mix of joy and terror I'll feel when we find out whether or not she's pregnant.

Long Shadow

LINDSAY ARRIVES AT my parents' house on Thursday a little before dinnertime, the day before Alexis's funeral.

"Hi," I say. I'm relieved to see her and we embrace for a long time, even though I am frantic over finishing the poster boards. I feel at ease in her arms, but also wary—like if I lean into the comfort too much I might fall over and never get up.

"When was the last time you showered?" Lindsay asks gently as we peel ourselves apart from one another.

"I don't know," I say, and for the first time I consider what I must look like. My hair is greasy. My body smells enough for even me to notice. I wonder if I look like I'm coming undone. Maybe I am. "I'm going to shower as soon as I finish."

"Do you need help?"

"No, I'm okay," I say. "There's a tray of hoagies in the fridge if you get hungry before dinner."

I go back down to the basement where I have boxes of photos to finish going through. I've bought five framed poster boards and my plan is to fill all of them with pictures of Alexis and quotes that she loved, but I'm only about halfway done.

I look at the partially completed boards and smile at the photo I've included of a pre-teen Alexis dressed for one of her dance recitals. She wears a royal blue leotard with a red bodysuit that shows off her lanky figure. Her blue eyeshadow is bold and overdone, as is her bright red lipstick. Underneath this photo I've written, *Alexis would probably want to kill me for including this*.

It's impossible to look at this image without laughing, and this is the very reason I chose it—to give people a place of lightness amidst the other heartbreaking images: a father next to his daughter on her first Halloween, a mother smiling down at her two girls on a trip to the pumpkin patch.

Between the photos on the board, I've copied quotes from a journal that Alexis kept, in which she meticulously hand-wrote quotes from various writers and organized them by theme: death, love, joy, friendship, art, beauty, and so on.

Near a photo of Alexis and our father at her dad-daughter dance, I copy part of Lewis Carroll's *The Jabberwocky*, which our father used to recite to us on long car rides when we were kids. His dramatic renditions always scared the shit out of us and we would squeal in terror as his voice rose and fell.

"'And hast thou slain the Jabberwock? Come to my arms my beamish boy! O frabjous day! Callooh! Callay! He chortled in his joy!'"

"How's it going?" Lindsay asks. I hadn't heard her coming down the steps and her voice startles me.

"Oh, hi. It's going. I can't find any pictures of Alexis with our Uncle Bill. I'm trying to have one of her with every family member, but I can't find any of the two of them and he's her godfather."

I show her some of the other contenders that I'm considering and watch her face expectantly as she looks at the photos, hoping for some sign of mild amusement or a slight fondness, but there is none, and the disappointment I feel is palpable.

"I feel conflicted over including pictures of me and Alexis," I tell her.

"What? Why?"

"It feels fake. I mean, we barely spoke over the last months. Our relationship was so strained, and now, what, I'm going to put pictures of us like this one on her funeral board?" I hold up an image from Alexis's 21st birthday where our arms are wrapped tightly around one another and our smiling faces are pressed cheek to cheek. There is no space between us in the photo. Space, back then, would've felt so foreign.

I recall the way that after my cousin Michael died of an overdose, I couldn't even bring myself to go up to his coffin at his viewing. I'd spent most of my time staring at all the photomontages that had been slapped together, thinking about how these collages were supposed to tell the story of a person's life, but they were a lie, or at the very least they were like looking through a crack in a fence at a person's life—offering only the most fragmented view. But they clearly brought people comfort in the face of terrible grief, so maybe it didn't matter if the portrait they painted was inaccurate.

"D," Lindsay says. "I think it's okay. You were close once."

"Yeah," I say, but I'm not convinced. The past days I've felt like a hypocrite every time I've cried over the loss of a sister whom I didn't even bother to call while she was alive and struggling. Why these tears now? Where were they when she was alive?

I go back and forth over whether to include photos of the two of us until I finally decide that a couple of pictures from childhood or high school would be okay because we were actually close back then.

I choose one of the two of us as young kids standing side by side in our frilly Easter outfits in front of our old dogwood tree and another of us sitting on her bed in an apartment she lived in one summer while she was in college. In this photo, one of her legs is draped across the front of my body and we both stare at the camera, unsmiling, both stoned out of our minds. The picture was taken just before we went downstairs to stuff our faces full of nachos that Alexis and her boyfriend had made in anticipation of our munchies.

I've always loved this picture. Whenever I look at it, I laugh at our stoned faces and I can't help but remember how much I adored and admired Alexis—her rebelliousness, her desire to expose me to new things whether that was pot or art or music, the way she managed to be both shy and completely attention-seeking at the same time by adding decorative flourishes to her outfits—a bright, furry scarf or a black leather jacket or unusual jewelry. When I look at this picture, I remember how big she was to me, how she cast such a long shadow, and the way that I was content for years to live in that shadow.

Now she is gone from this earth and "sister" has been erased from the list of words I have long used to explain my identity. Who am I now? Who am I without her?

Denial

DENIAL IS NOT the way I imagined it. It surprises me. It sits right next to the knowledge that my sister is dead and holds hands with it. The two things don't exclude one another or try to elbow each other out of the way, as I'd expected. They coexist peacefully, like old friends sitting on a bench watching the sunset.

The more time that passes, the more I comprehend that Alexis is dead, but I don't grasp the permanence—that she is not coming back. I have a little canister of her ashes on the windowsill in my bedroom. Once in a while, I unscrew the lid and touch them, then I rub my fingers on my skin like I'm applying perfume. *This is all that's left of your sister's body*, I tell myself. I understand, but I don't understand at all.

Thank You

"DID YOU CALL your sister to thank her for your wedding present?" my mother asks in November of 2012, a couple of months after Lindsay and I got married at the courthouse. She is perpetually trying to reunite Alexis and me. Handing me the phone unbidden whenever we are together and Alexis calls her.

"No, I sent her a card."

"A card? Well, aren't you going to call her?"

"No, we're not talking."

"Oh, you should really call her."

"Mom, she sends me awful, hateful text messages. I can't talk to her. It's not healthy for me."

"But you really should call her."

The Service

ON THE MORNING of the funeral, the limo is scheduled to come early to pick us up to go to the church. My Aunt Terry has come from New York for the service with her two twenty-something children, and the house is hectic with coordinating showers and getting dressed.

"Do you want to shower before me?" I ask my aunt.

"No, no, you go ahead. Where's the coffee?" I point to the last cabinet in the row where my parents keep their pod coffees. She retrieves one, but then stands there, unsure of what to do with it.

"Here." I grab the small container and put it in the machine for her, feeling a quick flare of anger at the fact that she needs to be shown how to do this. Clearly I am in a fragile emotional state. Aunt Terry is my favorite relative and I've never felt anything other than adoration for her.

After I shower, I change back and forth between pants and a skirt before finally listening to Lindsay who says that I will be cold in the church if I wear a skirt. The limo comes and we all scurry about, packing the poster boards in the trunk, along with a cardboard box filled with Alexis's artwork and a framed award certificate that she'd received for a story she'd written when she worked as a journalist.

At the church, I set the poster boards on easels that Colleen has brought from the funeral home. I move them around until I am happy with the order. Colleen brings in the urn. It's not the bright red I'd hoped for.

"Here," Colleen says, handing my mom and me each a cylindrical, white plastic container that is slightly larger than the ones used for old 35mm film. "Your ashes." It takes me a moment to process that Colleen has just handed me Alexis's cremains. I turn to my mother.

"Can you keep these in your purse?"

"Yes," she says as she gently tucks them into her bag.

I carry the urn up the aisle and place it on a small table. Next to it, we put the large photo of Alexis and the blow-up of the quote that she wrote, "So fragile we are—the sheets on the bed leave creases on our skin that fade to sight but not to soul."

Erin Riley brings the flowers. She has a large wreath that she places around the urn. "I don't like that," I tell my mother. "You can barely see the urn now! I want everyone to be able to see her." I say this as if Erin has just covered Alexis with a blanket. My mother nods in agreement and we both begin looking around for a solution.

I grab a couple of hymnals and place them underneath the urn, which raises it above the ring. "There," I say. I'm obsessing, I know, but I don't care. Each detail feels more important than the next. I keep thinking of Alexis watching all of this and about how much she'd love this whole thing, and about how sorry I am that she isn't here to see all the people who once loved her pouring into this church.

Over the last day and a half I have had the thought that the pressure of planning a funeral is similar to planning a wedding, only on a compressed time frame and for a far more depressing occasion. There are countless details and an intense desire for everything to be perfect, only there is no time to linger over decisions. No time to comparison shop. In the past day and a half I have run around from place to place, frantically checking things off of a long list of to-do's, and now I'm nervously skittering about, trying to ensure that things go smoothly, like some kind of deranged funeral planner.

Alexis would love all the attention that is being paid to each decision; she'd have something to say about even the tiniest details—like which quote we put on the mass card. If she were here, she'd be driving me fucking crazy. It would have taken her months to choose a quote because she'd have read 7,000 in search of the perfect one, then she'd have made a list of her favorites, all of which would have been too long to fit on such a small card, but there would have been no explaining that to her, no reasoning. She'd say something like, "Well this is my funeral, and I should get whatever I want," and who the hell could argue with that?

Eventually, people start streaming into the church's back doors. As I stand at the front of the church, receiving people, my leg twitches uncontrollably. Friends of my sister's from high school are suddenly standing in front of me, hugging me. When I see their faces, I am touched to the point of tears. More people flow in, offering condolences: my mother-in-law, my boss, one of Alexis's grade school teachers, cousins, aunts, uncles, great aunts, my mom and dad's co-workers. My four best friends come up the aisle and hug me for a long time, and then sit down in a pew next to where I stand. I see two of my friends from college walking up the aisle. I haven't seen or talked to them in years. Each familiar face overwhelms me a bit more.

Lindsay stands next to me and shakes hands with the

people in line. My father introduces us to the people we don't know. He doesn't hesitate or flinch when he says that Lindsay is my wife and I'm filled with gratitude at how far we've all moved since I came out to them at twenty-one. I feel steadier with Lindsay by my side. I think of the old clichéd love poems about marriage: if you fall I will catch you, when you are weak I will be strong.

I say thank you to each of the guests. I repeat over and over that Alexis had a rough time and I hope that she is resting easy now. When they pass us, they go up to her urn, where they linger awkwardly before turning around and finding a pew to sit in.

"My leg won't stop twitching," I tell Lindsay.

"Maybe you should eat something."

I blink. She walks over to my friends and comes back with a granola bar. I force myself to take a bite, but chewing feels like a great labor, like there is no saliva in my mouth. I'm handed a bottle of water and I take a sip, swish it around, and swallow.

Father Paul announces that the mass will begin soon and the line of people speeds up, whizzing by. As it reaches the end, the poster boards are whisked away by Colleen and her people, who come in quietly like a stage crew.

Aunt Terry makes her way up to the microphone and reads a poem, then Alexis's oldest friend, Michelle, delivers a eulogy. I can't focus on what either of them says, but I am conscious that people laugh a couple of times as Michelle speaks. My leg continues to twitch. Lindsay puts her hand on top of my knee. When Michelle finishes, I stand. I haven't really prepared anything to say other than stringing a few thoughts together in my head, because I haven't been able to bring myself to write anything. This is completely out of character for me, as I never speak off the cuff, but I feel compelled to say something, as if my silence would be a slap in the face to my dead sister.

"For those of you who don't know me, I'm Alexis's sister." I pause, clear my throat. "Alexis and I had a difficult relationship. When we were kids, we were really close, but as we got older and she got sick, I distanced myself from her. I was angry at her for a very long time because I thought that she was weak." My voice cracks and I know that I am going to have to finish this in that creepy voice that people talk in when they are trying to stifle tears.

"Yesterday, I was going through some of Alexis's things and I came across this bag filled with all the bracelets from her hospitalizations over the years. Some were for rehabs, some were for mental hospitals." Tears spill over my lower lid and stream down my cheeks. I pull the bag from my pocket where I'd stuffed it earlier that morning and I hold it up for people to see. "There must be twenty bracelets in here." The sound of someone blowing their nose is muffled by the local firehouse siren that begins a slow and mounting whir. "Alexis wasn't weak, she was strong. This is what it looks like to be strong. So if any of you here have someone in your life like Alexis, I hope you will be kinder to them than I was to her." My words are a warning, and I want to scream other words: *Don't be like me, you will be so sorry and you will have to live with your sorrow forever and you will not know how and you might not be able to, but you will have no choice, so don't be like me,* but a small, rational part of me knows this would be inappropriate and therefore remains silent.

I find my way back to my pew and sit down. Lindsay squeezes my hand. For the rest of the service I stand and sit and kneel at all the appropriate times. The responses have been programmed into me from years and years of going to mass. It is a small comfort to have this muscle memory lead my body that otherwise feels like it is floating in space.

When the service is over, I carry the urn down the aisle,

out the door, and into our waiting limo. As we begin the procession of cars that will go to the cemetery, my mother tells the driver that she wants to go past our old house and suddenly we are turning down our old street, passing the house where we grew up. A long line of cars snakes down Marshall Road and then turns right onto Lincoln Avenue. I haven't seen the house since my parents moved out nearly three years ago and as we pass it I notice that the front path that my father kept immaculate now has weeds poking out from the cracked mortar between bricks.

At the cemetery, the sun beats down on us and the older people are encouraged to sit under the tent. Father Paul says a few words about ashes to ashes, offers a prayer, and then someone from the funeral home signals for us to lay our roses on the urn. We are supposed to do this and then walk away, but I shake my head no. "I want to go last," I say firmly to no one in particular. So we sit and watch people place flowers—carnations and roses—on the urn. One by one.

When it is our turn we stand. My father places a few seashells on top of the pile of flowers. *Bring me back a seashell*, Alexis had told him before they left for Florida. My mother bends over the urn and kisses it. She looks so broken. A noise comes out of her, a sound reminiscent of an injured animal; a sound like the embodiment of suffering. My father and I hold her arms, taking her weight. She gurgles out that she loved her.

For a moment I think that my father and I might have to pull my mother off of the urn, but she straightens up and we help her off the platform that they have placed around the hole where my sister will be buried. I point at her urn. "You rest easy," I say. This is my wish for her: that wherever she is, things are easy and light.

It feels odd leaving the urn, as if we are abandoning her, and I want to turn back and take it with me, but the

Catholic religion requires burial. *She's dead*, I remind myself, *you can't abandon her anymore*. Then I remember the two small canisters of ashes in my mother's purse, which brings me so much comfort. It feels like we got something over on the Catholic Church by keeping them, like we are giving the middle finger to their rules, and I know that Alexis would most definitely approve.

Nice Lies

AFTER THE SERVICE ends, some people linger while others get in their cars and drive away. Lindsay stands next to me as I watch everybody disperse. She squeezes my hand. "Dylan told me to tell you that Alexis loved you, and that she knew that you loved her," she says. Dylan was one of my sister's close friends. I think he was in love with her, but I don't know how she felt toward him. Now it's too late to ask her. I squeeze Lindsay's hand to acknowledge what she's just said. I don't believe it, don't believe that Alexis could have possibly known that I loved her, but somehow it comforts me, the way I imagine a cup of water poured on a fire might give slight relief from the heat, even if it doesn't extinguish the flames. Sometimes lies are nice to hear.

At the Grave

The first weekend after the funeral, I take the train from Baltimore to be with my parents. On the way to visit Alexis's grave, we stop at The Home Depot. "She'd like this," I say, pointing to a glass rooster attached to a rod that stakes into the ground. We all laugh because it looks enough like a chicken, and Alexis loved to make startlingly loud be-gok noises at inappropriate times. It was one of the many ways her mischievous sense of humor came out. She also thought it quite funny to tap people on the shoulder while waiting in line and then act as if my father had done it. Once, when she'd done this to a man in front of us, the man grew angry when my father denied touching him, and Alexis had watched the whole thing play out while stifling her laughter.

The rooster has a small solar grid. It gives me a feeling of comfort when I think of it glowing next to her grave. I pull one out of the bin and we make our way to the line in the outdoor garden section. People in front and behind us have plants for their gardens and all the accouterments to help the plants thrive. Bags of soil, Miracle-Gro, and mulch are stacked on flat, orange carts. I imagine these people, tending their gardens, gently harvesting fruit or vegetables in a few months.

All around us things are bursting into bloom and it feels like a cruelty. Birds making nests in trees and emptying feeders in yards, the daffodils pushing up from the earth with the loose stance of a bored teen, the weeds exploding in flower beds—all of it a stunning betrayal because some part of me expected the earth to mourn with me, for things to slow down, but of course nothing does. I'll spend the summer cursing the grass each week when I see that it needs mowing. I'll glare out at it and think, *how dare you.*

When we arrive at her grave, Lynyrd Skynyrd's *Free Bird* blasts from the open windows of an idling truck. In a few months, someone will pick this song as the song that most reminds them of Alexis when I embark on making a book/ CD compilation in honor of her. We step out of the car as the truck rumbles off.

My parents have put a flag with an "A" here as a temporary marker, since there's no headstone yet. When they last visited the site, the marker had been removed and my mother stormed into the office demanding to know where it had gone. The staff informed her that they periodically clear the graves as a matter of policy.

"I know that!" she fumed, "but they told me that we could have a flag there until we get the stone!" They directed her to a dumpster that contained everything that got stripped off of the graves. She and my father had rooted through it until they found the flag. When my father had told me this story, the image of the two of them picking through the dumpster stuck with me, and it became a thing I circled back to when I needed a visual reminder of grief's many faces.

The three of us stand around the plot where the earth has begun to settle and sink, forming a small swale. This is a new ritual for the three of us and I find myself wishing for someone to instruct me on what to do with my body. My hands crave a task, so I lace my fingers together and press one thumb up against the other. The flowers from the service have turned brown.

"They need to get some more soil in here," my dad says, breaking the silence and pointing to the swale. He bends down and picks up the seashells that he had placed on top of her urn at the service. I imagine him bent over at the water's edge, picking up the prettiest shells he could find and stuffing them into his bathing suit pocket to bring home to her. He closes his palm around them and shakes, the way one would with loose change.

"How could you do this?" my mother says suddenly. I look over to where she's staring at the ground, shaking her fist angrily, then all at once, the tension goes out of her body and her arm drops to her side. "Oh, shit," she says, dissolving into tears. "It's just so fucking permanent."

My mother rarely curses and when she does, she doesn't say *fuck*. When she's really worked up, she says *frig* in this way that sounds silly enough to undercut her anger. Hearing her say *fuck* only reinforces the gravity of this moment. I drape my arm over her shoulder and squeeze. She lets out a breath and leans into me. My father steps forward and stakes the chicken into the ground.

"There," he says with satisfaction, but then he immediately begins tinkering with it, looking up at the sky. "Wait a minute, where will this get the most sun? Let's see, there's a compass on my phone somewhere." He digs into his pocket and stares at his screen, trying to determine which direction is east. My mother wanders off down the row of graves.

This past week my parents began shopping for a headstone. My mother called me to tell me that it was a good thing that they'd gone to more than one place because there was quite a difference in price. *Death*, I'd thought, *what a way to make a profit*. Cemetery plots, tombstones, caskets, cremation. All of it felt so absurd to me.

"Do you think this is the mahogany color stone?" my mother calls over to my father. He looks up from his phone and moves the chicken's solar grid with purpose, then directs his attention to my mother.

"Huh?"

"This stone," she says, "do you think this is mahogany?"

"Oh, well, let's see," he says, looking around at all the others. "Yeah, it must be."

"What do you think, Danielle? Do you like this color?" my mom asks.

"Um, yeah, it's nice," I say, trying to stay neutral since they are the ones who are going to be buried here alongside my sister and I feel no need to approve of their color choice. The cemetery is filled with different size monuments in a variety of colors and I can't help but feel that the whole process has disturbing parallels to car shopping. If you have enough money you can get a Mercedes with heated leather seats *and* a heated steering wheel, which makes the stone that juts out of the ground feel like some kind of status symbol for the dead, or worse, a supposed indicator of how much the dead person was loved. If it were up to me everyone would get the same stone, like in military cemeteries. No flourishes, no different sizes, just unending rows of sameness because we are all human and all valuable.

My father walks toward my mom and points to another one. "Do you think that's the large or the medium?"

"I don't know," my mother says thoughtfully.

"Damnit, I should've brought a tape measure. Wait, I might have one in my car!" My father hurries back to the car while my mom continues down the row, pointing out things she likes on certain stones.

"Oohh, this cross is beautiful," she says. My father emerges from the car carrying an ancient circular tape. He moves purposefully to where my mother is touching a stone. The tape clicks as he pulls it across the face. "Forty-two inches. This must be a medium."

"I think that's a nice size, don't you? Would the large be too big?"

I listen as they go back and forth over color and size, giving non-committal responses when they solicit my opinion. *Sure, yes, that's nice*, I say over and over half-heartedly. I look around at all the other stones, calculating the age of each dead person. 25, 72, 40, 7, 89. All dead. My sister, 42. Dead.

"I think we should do the mahogany. The grey is too plain."

"Yeah, I like the brown."

"What size do you think she'd want?" my mother asks.

My father and I look at one another, smiling, on the verge of laughter.

"LARGE!" we say in unison.

My dad launches into an impression of Alexis when we went out to restaurants. "I'll have a large and I'll take what I don't finish home with me."

We all laugh. Her eyes were always bigger than her stomach.

Relationship

"I FEEL LIKE you're not here with me," Lindsay says several months after Alexis's death. "Like part of you is somewhere else."

I sit next to her on our brown couch and do my best to listen and try to put myself in her shoes, to imagine what it would feel like to lose some part of her. We have begun the process of trying to have a baby, so she is craving closeness and I understand this, but I also feel angry. I want to scream, *My sister is dead, what the fuck do you expect?*

It's not that part of me is somewhere else, it's that part of me has been run over with a truck and even if my body makes a full recovery, even if my bones mend themselves, they will still sing to me when it's about to rain. How can I explain this?

I think of the way that fire changes things chemically. The way that there is no going back. The way that the cells of an object are broken down. I think of my sister's body. Of her ashes that I keep on my windowsill and kiss each night before bed.

I want to apologize to Lindsay for myself, for who I have become. I want to pretend, for her sake, that I will find a way back to the old me, but I know this is not true. I am a new version of me, a little worse for the wear, but maybe there's some beauty in this too. The phoenix rising from the ashes. The ashes, just a pile of what was once something else.

Support Group

A FEW WEEKS after Alexis's death, I make my way to my first support group meeting for survivors of suicide. The name of the group is Seasons and the room where it's held is small, with a loosely formed circle made out of chairs and a couple of couches. I choose a seat near the door and sit with my shoulders hunched and my eyes trained on the rug. All around the room, groups of two or three people are clumped together, talking quietly. Everybody seems to know one another. Someone laughs, which unnerves me.

The moderators are a married couple, Stan and Barbara, whom I emailed prior to the meeting. Stan had emailed me back quickly, expressing his condolences and telling me that he and Barbara had lost their son.

A woman approaches me and gingerly rests a hand on my shoulder. "I'm Barbara," she says. "I'm glad you came. I know it's hard. We call this, 'the club no one wants to join.'" She gives me a sad half-smile, then shows me where the nametags are and gives me a paper to fill out with the name of my loved one and the date of death.

I stare at it, but I'm unable to write anything. It feels too official. Too permanent.

"Okay everybody," Stan says. "We're going to get started."

People who had been milling around near the refreshment table make their way to their seats.

Stan launches into what is obviously a monthly spiel, explaining that the group has been around for thirty-plus years. When Stan stumbles in his speech, Barbara fills in the gaps, and he grins in an *oh shucks* way, as if he's come to rely on her. When he smiles, the tops of his cheeks take the shape of two small cherries. He exudes some sort of inner happiness that feels both out of place here and extremely reassuring.

I find myself wondering how the loss of Stan and Barbara's son has shaped their relationship. Part of why I've come here is to see what people who have survived loss look like, to glimpse the future of myself and my parents.

"Okay so we're going to have introductions followed by a ten-minute break and after that we'll start the meeting. If you're unable or don't want to speak, that's fine, you can just say pass."

Stan looks directly at me a couple of times as he says this. I nod my head to acknowledge him, but I'm confused over why there is a break so soon into the meeting. Why wouldn't it happen in the middle rather than ten minutes into a two-hour meeting?

"So we ask for three things during introductions," Stan says. "The name of your loved one, date of death, and the method used."

Oh God. I immediately begin mentally rehearsing the information so that I'll be ready when it's my turn. I know that I could pass, but something in me feels that I need to say it out loud.

Stan begins the introductions and then the person next to him goes. A son who shot himself, a husband who stabbed himself, a wife who overdosed, a daughter who hanged herself, a fiancé who shot himself in the head, a brother who hanged himself.

As each person shares about their loved one, scenes flash through my mind in which the loved ones discover the body. None of the group members mention anything about this during their intro, and yet I envision each person coming upon the body of their son or daughter. I hear them screaming and wailing.

A tiny, bird-like woman begins her introduction in a voice so quiet that I find myself leaning in, straining to hear. "I'm Sue. On June 19th, 2002, my husband, John, ended his life by hanging himself with his favorite belt while I was out getting groceries." My brain conjures an image of Sue waiting at the deli counter for her lunch meat while her husband wrapped a belt around his neck at their home. I can see her coming through the door with bags of food, calling to her husband for help.

"And," she says, "my son Frank ended his life with a gunshot wound on December 19th, 2011."

When I hear this, I'm stunned. Two suicides. My body feels as though it has melded itself to my seat. If someone came over to fold up the chair right now, my body would fold right up with it.

I always knew this was a possibility. A few years ago I met a friend who had lost two of her brothers to suicide, but somehow that double loss didn't register the same way with me as it does now. How does someone survive this? How can this tiny, bird-like woman contain so much grief in that small body? She seems both frail and unshakeable at the same time.

I want to stare and stare at her; to study her as if her body has a secret to tell me about getting through tragedy, but the next person in the circle has already begun and then it is my turn.

I take a breath. "My name is Danielle," I say. "My sister, Alexis, ended her life on May 23rd, 2016 by taking an intentional overdose. She was forty-two." My voice comes out monotone. I make sure to use the word "intentional" because it's important that no one here thinks her death was an accident, the way that my mother seems to.

After everyone has spoken, it feels as though an hour has passed, and when Stan announces the break, there's something of a collective exhale from the room, which makes me aware that we'd all been holding our breath. Now the break makes perfect sense.

When the meeting resumes, a woman with long, straight brown hair and piercing blue Wonder Woman eyes begins sharing about the loss of her daughter. The woman is perilously thin and fidgets constantly, pulling at her sleeve and at the strap on her watch. Her voice shakes as she talks about her husband and her other children; about how she is no longer present for them; about how one of her daughters is angry with her because she feels like she lost both a sister and a mother. The woman's brow is creased in a grimace that looks permanent, as if her face has been molded by her pain and then cast in bronze.

As I listen, I feel both at home and out of place in the group. Since we've all lost someone to suicide, there's no stigma. We are all equals in that regard; all marked by a loss that most people on the outside don't know how to react to, but my grief feels small and bearable compared to the people who have lost their child.

What is my grief next to this woman's? It is nothing. It is tiny, manageable, a thing I can hold in my palm and roll around like a marble, and put away when I need to do the things of life—work, go to the store, pay bills. This woman's grief is a large boulder that demands carrying. It requires every ounce of her energy to keep it from crushing her. She has nothing left for anyone else. Not even her other children.

When it gets close to the end of the meeting, Barbara looks at me and says, "Danielle, is there anything that you'd like to share?"

I consider a simple "no," but when I open my mouth, other words come out.

"I, um, well, my sister and I didn't have the best relationship. She was sick for a long, long time and she could be really hard to love. I mean, *really* hard. She had addiction issues and Bipolar Disorder and she tried to end her life so many times that I lost count, so I've been expecting this for years, but somehow when my dad called me to tell me, I was completely shocked. My parents went away for their 46th wedding anniversary and when they came back, they found her." I pause. My thoughts are coming faster than I can process.

"And for all these years, I was so angry with her, but now it's like all of my anger towards her is gone, and I can see that she was so strong to have survived as long as she did. I would have been dead so much sooner if I had her brain. I would have given up sooner."

I ramble for another minute, weaving in and out of the past and the present, and when I stop, I let out a long breath. People respond with kind comments and I try to take in what they are saying, but none of it sticks.

At the end of the meeting, I leave feeling heavier and lighter, as if I've agreed to carry a piece of these strangers' grief and they've accepted a small portion of mine. I also feel relieved to know that there are others who understand the loneliness of grief—the way that it is yours and yours alone to hold and knead in your hands and to see if it will be a thing that destroys you or whether it will be a thing that gives rise to beauty.

I still feel utterly alone, but knowing that there are others who are walking the same kind of path, even if in a different forest, I feel the tiniest bit better.

One Month After

My phone rings one morning as I unlock the door to the cabinet shop where I work. It's been two and a half weeks since I came back and I'm still trying to catch up on all the things I left undone when I got the phone call about Alexis. I'm the first one here today and the air smells of the familiar blend of sawed wood that I've come to think of as home.

"Hi Mom," I say.

"Are you at work?"

"Yeah, I'm just walking in."

"Oh, I can call you later."

"No, no, I can talk for a bit."

"Are you sure?"

"Yes, it's fine. How are you?"

I walk into the kitchen and put my lunch in the fridge. In the weeks since my sister's death, I've been desperate for contact with my parents. Before Alexis died, there were times when I was too busy to answer phone calls from my mom and dad, but this feels unimaginable now.

"I'm okay," she says. "How about you?"

"Alright."

This is how most of our conversations go. We dance around our emotions, waiting for the other one to open up; afraid to be the first to say we are struggling. Even though I yearn for daily contact with my parents, it's hard to know how to talk to one another these days. If we keep things light it feels false, but we are both hesitant to delve deep. We're like scared children, afraid to jump off the high dive until we see the other go first, but today my mother leaps.

"I've been meaning to tell you that I know what you're going through."

Immediately, I know she is referring to her brother, Danny, who was stabbed and killed when he was in his twenties. I am his namesake. She rarely talks about his death, and never without prompting. Most of the details I know have been gleaned from conversations with my father and other relatives.

As the story goes, Danny had been out at a bar where he met up with two guys he knew from the Fairmount neighborhood of Philadelphia. When the bar closed, they went to an after-hours club with two young women they'd met. At the club, there was an argument that turned violent in the parking lot. Danny was stabbed and then he tried to make his way to the nearby police station, but collapsed along the way. He was found and rushed to the hospital where he died.

On the news, the story of the stabbing circulated. Danny's family worried when he didn't come home Sunday, but tried to explain it away. The body of the unidentified man on the news couldn't be their Danny. But by Monday, the police had somehow made the connection and called my mother, who was home with four-month-old Alexis.

Uncle Marty, who was a police officer, drove my mother over to the morgue to identify her brother's body. Of all the things that my mother has done in her life, this is the one that most perfectly represents her unmatched strength—getting in a police car to go stare at the face of her dead brother, because she refused to leave this task to her parents or her brothers.

I'm the first one to arrive at the cabinet shop today and as I walk into the paint room, I flip the light switch and make a mental note to change the fan filter, as it is caked with dust. Later, I will don a respirator and spray cabinet doors while the fan works to pull the vapor out of the air. I have somehow become the de facto finisher for our small shop, a job I previously despised, but ever since Alexis died, I have found comfort in the mindlessness of the work. And when I'm doing it, I don't have to worry about cutting off a finger with a power tool.

"On the day that we found out about Danny," my mother explains, "your father and I went over to your Grandpop's work to tell him. When we got out of the car, he saw us and asked if it was Danny, and when I said yes, he just collapsed onto the ground." She pauses as if catching her breath, as if the memory of it still shocks her. "My father was a big, strong man, and he just fell to the ground."

My mind flashes to the moment that my parents found Alexis's body. It's a scene I have imagined countless times.

I don't know what to say to my mother, so I just listen, waiting for her to continue. I begin to straighten the gallons of paint on the counter. Five different shades of white, three greys—all the most recent trends in kitchen colors.

"I remember feeling like I would do anything to take away their pain," she says, "and I know that's how you feel. The hardest part of losing Danny was watching my parents hurt so much."

I am quiet for a moment as I fiddle with the spray gun in the finish room. Hearing my mom say this, I feel seen. Since

Alexis died, my heart has broken for them in ways that it never did for Alexis when she was alive. Perhaps my mom understands this. Perhaps she'd been angry with her brother for the choices he'd made on the night he'd been killed. Perhaps part of her had been swallowed by anger toward Danny just as part of me had been with Alexis. I feel relieved knowing that she's been where I am, but before the relief has a chance to settle in, I realize for the first time that my mother has lived through the loss of a sibling, and now the loss of a daughter.

At the Church

WHEN I ARRIVE at my writing residency, I crane my neck to take in the spire that juts skyward from "the church" where I'll spend the next two weeks. According to the information packet emailed to me some months before, this building was the second property purchased by the Ora Lerman Trust. A few miles away, there's a house that can host four residents simultaneously, as opposed to the church's capacity of two. When presented with the option of staying at the church or the house, I requested to stay here because I knew I'd be more likely to be alone, and the idea of aloneness was appealing in the abstract.

The last residency I'd attended was on a farm in Nebraska, appropriately named Art Farm. There had been a handful of other artists there with me, and while it was a comfort to have people to commune with, particularly when every other thing in my external environment—from the kitchen utensils to the shared bathrooms to the way the Nebraska wind rattled the house at night—was foreign and unfamiliar, I'd discovered that having people around allowed me to avoid looking inward. I'd find myself down in the kitchen or in the room with the wood-burning stove, hoping that one of the other residents would be around and want to hang out for a while. After that experience, I decided that being completely alone and quiet was necessary for me to truly face the parts of myself that I'd be more comfortable keeping at a distance.

But the moment I open the door of the church, I wonder whether this was the wrong decision. Under the strain of my grief, things that I always considered pillars of my identity— that I am strong, solid, stable—have become things I question. Most days, it feels like there is as much of a chance that I will fall apart as there is that I will keep it together. A wave of fear so much more intense than I'd imagined when I'd decided to opt for the church overwhelms me. It feels like a block of ice has been plunked inside my ribcage. The cold rises into my throat. Once, when Alexis was in college, she told me about her experience with trying acid. She cautioned me to never try it unless I was in a really positive mental space, because she said that any hint of darkness in one's mind could send a person on a nightmare of a trip, rather than a psychedelic, relaxing one. I wonder whether the same rules apply to being alone when in the throes of a guilt-tinged grief.

It's too soon to be alone, I think, but even as the thought comes, I know I won't leave. I deserve any dose of discomfort or unease that arises here. Alexis had felt lonely, scared, and uncomfortable for much of her life and, five months out from her death, I still feel that I hadn't done enough to help ease those feelings for her. I flash to the conversation we'd had on Easter, when Alexis had regaled me with a litany of woes, and I had offered empty words of sympathy. The least I can do now is to understand, empathize—a penance of sorts. I take a deep breath, hoping it will calm my fluttering heart.

As I step into the space, I look around, trying to find some source of comfort. Downstairs doesn't resemble a church at all. On either side of the main entrance are a bedroom and a small bathroom. A circular dining table sits just off of a galley-style kitchen in a multipurpose room. This room also houses a small couch, a bookshelf full of art books, and a pair of French doors that lead to a rickety side porch with a spectacular view of the adjacent farmland. Beyond that, there are hills covered with trees at the peak of their fall colors. The church property backs up to a fenced-off pen full of goats.

A large studio occupies the second level. It's a high-ceilinged affair with splatters of paint on the hardwood floor and a bed shoved into a small loft area. An easel, a small desk, and a shelf unit cluttered with old paintbrushes and rags are the only other furnishings. Multiple windows allow for lots of natural light. I contemplate sleeping up here, but the empty openness unsettles me. Downstairs has a much homier feel, so as I begin unloading the car, I put my bags in the bedroom and then busy myself with housekeeping chores to try to quiet the unease that's buzzing through my veins like an electric current.

I set about making a vegetarian chili that will be my dinner for the better part of a week. I search for a knife to chop the onion and peppers that I picked up at a local market on my drive here. My sister's long-ago words come back to me from the Thanksgiving night she cut her wrist, "I've always loved the knives here," and my body tenses as I scan the drawer. All the knives are dull, so I grab the longest one and begin dicing. *I'll start writing tomorrow*, I think. *Today, just focus on making food and maybe read for a while before going to bed.*

After all the ingredients are in the pot, I leave the chili simmering and walk out the French doors and across the yard to where the goat pen begins. Two thin, spindly goats approach cautiously, while three heartier-looking ones stay back near a wooden climbing structure.

"Hi," I say to the two eyeing me curiously. I'm very self-conscious about the fact that I'm talking to goats, but I feel a need to speak out loud, even though I've only been by myself for a few hours. "How are you? I'll be your neighbor for the next couple of weeks." One of them maa's at me. "Yeah, I know. You were probably hoping for someone cooler, but you got me."

Talking to the goats quiets the buzzing inside of me, so I stay out for a few minutes, even though I feel foolish. Further back in the pen, one of the larger goats with a set of horns and a beard bleats continually at the other two in a bullying way, chasing them around. "What's Big Daddy's problem?" I ask the two near the fence. They study me and I am surprised by how much solace I take in their eyes.

It's around four by the time the chili is cooked and I turn off the stove to let it cool. I go into the bedroom to unpack. I take the canister of Alexis's ashes out and place it on the desk tucked in the corner, then turn to make the bed. Just as I am about to cover the mattress with a sheet, I see a dark blur dart across the bed. *Oh God*, I think, *no no no no no. Please don't be a spider*, but I already know it is. The blur has run out of sight and I upend the mattress, frantic to find it because, if I don't, I will not sleep one wink. It scurries toward the corner and I grab my nearby boot and slam it down so hard that a loud thud drowns out the sound of the crunching body. Immediately, I'm filled with regret. At home I would've trapped this creature in a glass and slid paper under the rim and then carried it outside to set it free, but here I am on edge, steered by fear. I get a paper towel and ball it up, trying not to look as I pinch the squished body into it. *You're in the country*, I tell myself, *there are bound to be some bugs here*. I finish unpacking, trying to shake the whole thing off, but when I go into the bathroom to hang my towel, there's an overturned body of a large wolf spider and my heart begins to pound again, even though this one is already dead. How many more are there in here? I sweep the body into a dustpan, doing my best not to visualize how large this thing would be if it wasn't curled up.

I grab my keys and drive to the nearest hardware store, where I buy a gallon of bug spray. When I get back, I soak the inside perimeter of the entire church, hoping that the spray will assuage my fears enough to let me sleep, then I heat some chili and sit at the table, my eyes scanning the floor continuously for any signs of movement. The sweet smell of the spray hangs in the air.

At bedtime, I perform what will become a nightly ritual. I shake out a pair of shorts and a T-shirt before putting them on. Next, I pick up the mattress and peer under it, then shake the sheet and sleeping bag. I turn the sleeping bag inside out, then shake it again before putting it right side out. I kiss my hand and touch the canister containing Alexis's ashes, and then slide my body inside the sleeping bag. If I have to get out of bed to pee, I know that I'll have to perform the whole elaborate ritual over, or else I'll think any sensation on my skin is a spider.

I'm too afraid to sleep in the dark here, so I leave the nightstand light on. As I stare at the ceiling, I begin to wonder whether the church is a safe place to stay. I consider that I'm in a rural town, and I wonder whether the locals know that this is a place where a woman might come to stay alone. I consider what would I do if I heard someone rattling a door or window. My body jumps with each unfamiliar noise or tick of the house. I'm enveloped by my fear. I think of the way that tree roots sometimes wrap so tightly around pipes that they crack them right open and I drift off wondering whether my own fear could do this to me. My sleep is fitful and hot inside the sleeping bag, but I don't dare to unzip it or climb out to go to the bathroom.

I wake damp and sweaty in the morning and I reach for my shoes because I'm damn sure not going to walk around in my socked feet. A large wolf spider the size of a silver dollar scurries out from underneath my sneaker. "Goddamnit motherfucker!" I shout, throwing the shoes in the air. I grab my boot and slam it down on the spider's body, breathing hard.

Later that morning, I call Lindsay and tell her about the spiders, but I downplay my fear, as though it's a laughable thing, a small nuisance and not a completely disruptive force. "I had myself zipped so tightly into my sleeping bag last night that I was drenched by morning," I say as if it's the most humorous thing.

As the week wears on, I find more bodies of spiders, but only see a couple of small living ones, and these don't elicit the same raw fear in me as the larger ones. My fear reduces in tiny gradients and I settle into a bit of a routine, writing in the morning, going for a walk midday, visiting with the goats, and then writing out on the porch while the sun sets over the far- off hills.

When I come inside one night, I page through several of Alexis's books where she organized her art cutouts. Since I received the white canister of Alexis's ashes on the day of her funeral, I've thought the container was too plain. I brush Mod Podge on a picture of Marilyn Monroe and glue it on the lid. On the side, I choose a heart that says *forget me not*. I agonize over the positioning of each piece I attach, trying my best to achieve some kind of balance. Each image brings me a slight sense of ease because it feels like I'm doing something Alexis would approve of. She'd want something beautiful on the outside of the thing that contains all that was left of her in this world.

Lindsay calls one evening toward the end of the first week. She sounds upset. "What's up?" I ask.

"Last night, Meg asked me if it would be okay if Carly came over to watch the debate and even though I didn't really want to say yes, I did."

The previous night, I'd plugged in an old radio and found a staticky station that was covering one of the Hillary Clinton versus Donald Trump debates.

"Okay, that's weird. How was it?"

"At first it was fine. We all watched together, and it was kind of fun to have people to laugh with about the ridiculousness. They were drinking wine and I went to bed. Then later, I heard them having sex. Like, multiple times. Meg didn't even ask if it was okay for her to stay over."

"What?! I'm gonna talk to her."

I think of Lindsay in our room being kept awake and I feel furious with Meg. Ever since the insemination a week ago, I've felt protective of Lindsay in a way that is completely foreign to me. The role of protector has never been one that either Lindsay or myself has felt compelled to occupy, maybe because we are two women in a relationship or maybe because we both view the other as capable and competent, but whatever the reason, I'm unfamiliar with this urge to shield Lindsay from any negativity.

"NO! You're away and I am the one dealing with this and I don't want you talking to Meg on my behalf. I just needed to vent," she says firmly.

I feel as though Lindsay has just tied my wrists together and asked me to bear witness to her suffering, and it aggravates me slightly. I want to fix any problem that arises, to make her path easy, but she wants none of this from me.

"Fine," I say. "But I'm pissed. That's so rude."

We both wait a beat, unsure what to say to alleviate the tension that has entered our conversation. "When do you go for the pregnancy test?" I ask.

"On Wednesday," she says.

"And then when do we hear?"

"I'm not sure, but it won't be long. How's your writing going?" Lindsay asks.

"Okay," I say. "I mean, I'm writing, but it's hard to say how it's going."

When we hang up, I consider dialing Meg, if for nothing else than to tell her that Lindsay might be pregnant, and that she'd better not stress her out, but I know this would only anger Lindsay, so I try to go back to my writing, which in truth is a mess. I can't imagine that it will ever amount to anything worthwhile. I'm trying to get the facts and details about Alexis's death down on the page, but I'm writing the way I always do, without any real structure or direction, trying to stay organized, but failing to do so. This is the same way I work when I undertake any creative endeavor, whether it's cooking or building cabinets. I start with a loose idea and a tentative plan, but before I know it, there are tools or spices and oils spread before me and I don't even remember taking them out, and I find myself in the middle of the process staring at the mess, hoping against hope that I can turn it into something beautiful or at least edible.

The day before I am scheduled to drive home, Lindsay calls me.

"Stephanie called," she says excitedly. "There's a voicemail."

Stephanie is our nurse at Shady Grove. The message has to be about the results of the pregnancy test.

"Should we listen to it? Or wait until I'm home?" I ask.

"I don't think I can wait," Lindsay says.

"Me neither," I say.

"Well, how should we do it?"

"Call me back on the home line and we can listen together," I say.

A moment later my phone rings. "Are you ready?"

"Yes," I say, even though I'm not.

"Hello Lindsay, this is Stephanie with Shady Grove calling to let you know that the results from your test were positive. Congratulations."

I don't hear the rest after that.

"Holy shit," I say. All of the trepidation I've experienced since coming to stay at the church seems suddenly microscopic. Stephanie's words ignite inside of me, a pilot light of fear that feels so much more substantial than anything I've felt here: fear of being a mom, fear of not being enough. But more than that, fear of losing this being—just a small cluster of cells at this point—whom I cannot touch or see, whom I can barely imagine, but whom I already love deeply and without reservation. I know this pilot light will burn for as long as our child is alive, and this knowledge ushers in a reverence for the flame. For the rest of my days I will nurture it, tend to it, shelter it. I will do anything to keep it burning.

What I Learn From the Autopsy: Everything and Nothing

The Everything:

How much Alexis's organs weighed in grams.

Whether those organs were easily removable.

The clothes she was wearing when she died, including descriptions of her underwear and bra.

That no palpable masses of her breasts were appreciated.

The color and consistency of the contents of her stomach.

The length of her hair from the apex of her head.

The location and description of each tattoo on her body.

The condition of her fingernails.

The color of the body bag she was placed in for transport.

The exact position her body was found on the floor, including the direction her head faced, the placement of each arm and leg.

That the rigor in her arm was easily broken.

The location of bruising on her body.

That there was a barrette in her hair and grey, chipping polish on her toes.

When I learn the Everything, I want immediately to unlearn it, even though for two months I have been hungry for it, so much so that during nearly every conversation with my parents I've asked whether the report had come or whether they'd heard anything new about the report, because I'd believed that it would bring the fuzzy picture of how Alexis died into tight and crisp focus. I thought that it would answer all of my lingering questions. It does not.

Instead, when I read the report, a movie reel plays in my head in which a stranger hovers over my sister's body, undresses her, and catalogs the details: cream-colored sweater, Eagles T-shirt, Calvin Klein bra. I watch the stranger measure her hair, inspect her nails, open her mouth to check her teeth as if she were some kind of animal. I want to scream for him to stop, but I know that he will only stop if I quit reading and I cannot tear my eyes from these pages. He scribbles down notes deeming her nails and teeth well cared for.

When he sees the scars on her left wrist, he does not caress them gently as I would; he gets his tape measure and holds it over them, then bends over and writes: "multiple transversely oriented to angled linear scars involving a total area of approximately 2 ⅛" transversely x 1 ¾", likely indicative of remote suicidal-type gesture."

I feel insulted by the words "remote suicidal-type gesture" as if her previous attempts on her life were not serious, as if she were just playing around all those times she ran a razor over her wrist, but before I can process this, the stranger grabs his scalpel, cuts my sister's chest open, cracks her ribs, and begins weighing her organs: liver, kidneys, spleen, heart. He deems her heart to be "of the appropriate overall configuration and size for her weight," which again feels like an insult because her heart was large and anything but ordinary.

In her stomach, he finds tan meat fragments as well as green and clear onion fragments. *Her last meal*, I think, shocked that this information feels so clinical and yet so intimate at the same time. The stranger also finds numerous round white tablets and larger yellow pills labeled "XR 300." I wonder whether the fact that the labels are still discernible means that she was dead before her body could even begin to absorb the full dose of pills she'd swallowed.

Then he is onto her skull, cutting through it with some kind of whirring blade until he can reach in, remove her brain, and hold it in his gloved hands. The brain that wrote lines of beautiful prose; that heard voices that didn't exist and saw shadowy images of creepy clowns in her bedroom; that invented a kingdom of magical fish to entertain me as a child. The brain that created too much of one chemical and not enough of another. The brain she tried so desperately to alter with medication and to quiet with alcohol.

I see her beautiful, horrid brain in the hands of this stranger, and I want desperately to take it from him, so that I can handle it with the care it deserves, this organ that made her who she was.

The Nothing:

Whether she had planned it out or decided on a whim.

Whether she was afraid as she lay dying.

Whether her death was painful.

Whether she regretted it.

Whether she knew that I loved her.

Whether she hated me more or less than she loved me.

The Nothing is worse than the Everything.

When I turn the fourteenth and final page over, I feel a deep disappointment settle in my bones—a heavy door slamming in my face. I'd been counting on this report to illuminate everything so brightly that even the tiniest particles of dust floating through the air would be visible, but it's little more than a dim bulb in a dark room and I feel momentarily betrayed by it, a feeling that is quickly overshadowed by the realization that I'd been a fool to expect the kinds of answers I had. The biggest revelation that has come from reading this report is that my dead sister is really dead.

Cause vs. Manner of Death

A QUICK GOOGLE search to find out the difference between *cause* and *manner* of death reveals that cause refers to the disease or injury that caused a disruption leading to death, whereas manner refers to how the death came about. A gunshot wound, for example, would be a cause of death, but the manner of death in the case of a gunshot wound could be an accident, homicide, or suicide, depending on the circumstances.

In my sister's autopsy report, the cause of death says: mixed benzodiazepine and ethanol ingestion complicated by probable positional asphyxia. But in the box for manner of death, typed in all capital letters, is the word UNDETERMINED. Not suicide, as I had expected.

I read these two things over and over, trying to decide whether they are part of the Everything or the Nothing.

Office Space

Lindsay and I are clearing out our office so that we can turn it into a baby's room. We are throwing things away, donating and organizing. Piles of paper line the floor. In one of the many stacks I find a sleeve of photos.

There is one of Alexis and me. She wears deep red lipstick, and her blonde hair is pulled to one side, fastened with a barrette. She looks to be on the verge of laughter.

"She looks so healthy here," I say, showing the photo to Lindsay. "This was before she went to rehab for the first time. It's hard to believe that was seventeen years ago."

Lindsay studies it for a moment and offers a slight smile before going back to sorting her stack. When she does this, I realize how desperately I wanted to hear her say, "Yes, she looks beautiful." But Lindsay is focused on the task at hand, looking ahead to our future, and I cannot blame her. I want to fix my eyes there too, but I can't. I keep looking back, as if to let Alexis and myself know that I haven't forgotten her.

Parents

IN THE WAKE of Alexis's death, my father becomes impatient with the rate at which my mother is capable of getting rid of her stuff. Though he doesn't say it, I gather he's desperate to make the loss less visible, and in his mind there is a structured way to do this—a series of steps that need to be taken. First and foremost is the restoration of physical order.

My father is a scientist who has always kept his emotions at a distance by looking at them through a lens of logic and rationality. I imagine him taking scrapings of his feelings and smearing them onto a glass slide, then peering through a microscope to study them, as if this could lessen their potential for devastation.

My sister's old room has become the main point of contention between my parents. My father wants it emptied out; my mother wants to save everything. For the most part, my father is winning this battle. *The room*, as we have all come to refer to it, perhaps because it's too painful to include Alexis's name, has been mostly emptied.

Each time my parents drop a load of boxes off at the local

thrift store, my father appears to feel lighter and less burdened, while my mother seems stripped—each disappearance another loss, an erasing.

When I talk to my mother on the phone, she complains about my father. "I don't know why he's in such a rush. What's the goddamn rush?" she says. "Once we get *the room* cleaned out, who's coming?" Her voice rises. "When all the stuff is gone, that's it. There's no more!"

"I know, Mom," I say softly. "I think it's just hard for Dad to look at all of her stuff. You both need to understand where the other one is coming from and talk to each other about it."

"He won't change," she says. "Give him a call, will you?"

I cringe at this request, but I know I'll do it anyway. I'm keenly aware that I'm acting as an emotional interpreter for my parents in a way that is unhealthy, but I don't know what else to do. When one of them complains to me, I feel it's my duty to explain what the other is probably going through. I'm afraid that without me there to translate their actions, they'll grow angry and resentful of one another. Like it's my job to save them from each other. I call my father and ask him how things are going.

"Mom wants to talk about Alexis every night," he says. "She's asked me why I don't talk about her more. I want to get *the room* emptied out and repainted," he continues. "I need to spackle the walls. Alexis had so many damn holes in the walls." He lets out a half-hearted laugh.

I think of how painful this will be for my mother—to see the traces of her daughter gone, the holes literally filled.

"If your mother would pick out a rug, we could get that taken care of too," he continues. "But she keeps changing her mind. Just the other day she told me that now she wants to get hardwoods in there. I told her no, to just pick out a rug."

My mind flashes to the rug that is in the room now. The discoloration that exists in the spot where Alexis died—a swath of green and yellow, almost blue. Part of me can't wait until it's gone, but part of me wants to save it, to cut out that patch and frame it, hang it on the wall, turn the house into a museum dedicated to Alexis's life and death. This would be the pièce de résistance. I wonder if my mother feels this way too.

In many ways, the house has already started to take on a museum-like quality. My sister's art covers the mantel and bookshelf downstairs. The huge photo that was blown up for the funeral mass has been set on top of a table in the entryway. The garage is filled with boxes from Alexis's storage unit. My last visit to their home filled me with a deep weariness because everywhere I turned, my eyes landed on a reminder of my dead sister.

"Dad, I think that every time you get rid of something, Mom feels like you're throwing away pieces of Alexis. You guys have to find a middle ground that you both can live with."

I've wondered whether my father feels the tiniest fraction of relief over the death of his daughter. This would be the most forbidden emotion for him, the most inexpressible—relief over not having to come home to the great unknown, to not have to listen to her rambling monologues at dinner, to not have to worry about her anymore. To say any of that would be impossible, but it occurs to me that he might feel it, right alongside his deep ache to see her again, his ache to make things right between them.

"I wish I could go back," he says. "I wish I could have another chance, but I can't." He sighs resignedly. "The only thing I can do is live my life."

I'm surprised by the difference in the ways that my parents' grief has begun to manifest. The intellectual part of me understands this as normal, but it's difficult to see each of them ripped open and neither able to tend the other's wounds. Their relationship has always seemed unshakeable in spite of the fact that there has long been a divide right down its very center—a solid spike of steel made up of the many disagreements they've had over the years about how to best help their very sick, adult child.

Where my father believed that boundaries and discipline might save Alexis, my mother believed that unconditional love and care were the way to go. But even when my father disagreed with my mother's approach, he generally accepted it as their practice, mostly out of an unspoken fear that if they'd instituted a tough love approach that resulted in Alexis's death, they'd never forgive themselves.

This wedge between them was a thing they'd grown accustomed to, a familiar object that they knew how to move around with relative ease. In Alexis's absence, the differentness in their grief is like a hammer bearing down on that metal spike, and I've found myself wondering how long a thing can hold together against such forceful blows.

Dream

WHEN I GO to bed, I dream of Alexis. In one dream, I am working at a restaurant as a hostess. It's a busy night at the restaurant and I'm trying to seat people, but when I take them to their table I find that it's filled with crumbs and dirty plates. I run back to the hostess station and there is another couple waiting to be seated and Alexis is there too. She looks beautiful and healthy.

Her hair is pulled back, swept up off of her neck, and she is dressed impeccably. We kiss hello and I am genuinely happy to see her, but I'm stressed about the seating situation, so I run back to the couple I've left near the dirty table. I get so wrapped up in my work that I forget all about my sister until much later in the night, when things have calmed down and I go searching for her.

I find her sleeping on the bench right near my hostess stand and, by now, she looks different, disheveled. I wake her. She is out of it and I suspect drugs. I have the vague notion that she has transformed, that she is not the put-together woman I saw a couple of hours ago. I'm filled with the sense that I want to go back. Back to a few hours ago, back to when she looked so healthy.

The First Holiday

My mother has been actively avoiding the subject of Thanksgiving and I've been trying to be sensitive to her needs, but the anxious planner in me has gotten too impatient. Lindsay, too, has gotten atypically impatient about setting our plans in stone. I've chalked this up to the tiredness that's been brought on in the first trimester of her pregnancy because, as the youngest of four girls, she's usually adept at going with the flow. We are keeping the news of the pregnancy to ourselves until Lindsay is closer to twelve weeks. We don't want to instill hope into anyone, especially my parents, until after this milestone, when the chances of a miscarriage drop significantly.

When I finally call to pin down my mom on our plans, she and my dad are at Lowe's looking for new chairs for the deck.

"The old ones are falling apart," she says.

"Yeah, I know," I say, remembering how I sat in those wicker chairs the week after Alexis died, picking at the loose pieces and pulling them from the woven tangle as I made phone calls to inform people of her death.

"Mom," I say now, "I'd like to talk about Thanksgiving sometime soon." I let out a deep breath. It feels good, as if this is a kindness on my part to give my mom a heads up about the fact that I want to have this conversation in the near future, as if giving her time to prepare will make it easier.

My mother says nothing for several moments and I wait, uncomfortable with the silence, but unsure what else to add.

"Okay," she finally says with a cracking voice. I close my eyes and squeeze my free hand into a fist, imagining my mother standing in the high-ceilinged store, tears streaming down her face, surrounded by outdoor furniture. It feels like both the saddest and the most cliché thing in the world—something Hollywood would put in a movie to demonstrate to an audience that a character is grieving. Something that so fully represents grief, and yet doesn't do it justice in the least.

"Mom, I'm sorry. We don't have to talk now."

I think of how grief is so much bigger than those singular, dramatic instances; how it's all the moments in between, like when you get up and go to work and type on your computer and answer the phone while inside you are dying. It's the moments that you aren't crying.

I imagine grief like a tree that grows inside of you, shedding leaves and then growing them back. A thing that can be lighter, and then heavier; bare, and then full; a thing that can bloom and then wither; that can sprout shoots that may turn into thick branches. A thing that changes every day, as if each day inside of us is its own season.

When I think of my mother's grief, I envision one of those giant old sycamore trees taking up all the space inside of her, its roots drawn tight around her heart, its impossibly heavy branches casting long shadows.

I picture my mom in the Lowe's hanging up her cell phone, returning it to her purse, and then continuing with the shopping excursion. I see her walking through the store as her grief bears down on her, but walking anyway, because what other choice does she have?

The First Holiday: Take Two

MY MOTHER'S OLDEST brother, Bill, has become a hermit since losing his son, Michael, to an overdose. My Uncle Bill had never been the picture of mental health. He'd been wounded in the Vietnam War and had PTSD that went mostly untreated. Now, he holes up in his room and spends his entire day on his computer.

"Maybe we should go to the shore," my mother says. "If we go there, Cameron will have a Thanksgiving. Otherwise he won't." We are on the phone again and finally talking about plans for the holiday, but my mother cannot make up her mind. My mother and father have a shore house around the corner from my Uncle Bill, outside of Cape May, New Jersey, and Cameron is Michael's teenage son, whom my Uncle Bill and his wife Maryann adopted after Michael died.

I do not want to spend this Thanksgiving with my Uncle Bill and I wish that my mother would stop thinking about everyone else for ten seconds and just focus on what she wants. Why would she choose to spend the day around a brother who is trapped in his grief? What's more, I don't think I can handle staring down the face of what grief can do to a person, especially a parent.

"Mom," I say as gently as I can, "I think that for this first year, this first holiday, you should just focus on you and what you're able to do. I mean, it's going to be hard enough without adding all of those other layers."

"Well truthfully, I don't know if I'm even going to want to get out of bed on Thanksgiving."

"If that's what you need, that's what you should do," I say without hesitation, but a small part of me is wounded by these words.

My mother is not the kind to give in to anything, not the kind to stay in bed all day, no matter the circumstance. So I don't actually believe her when she says this, but for a moment I entertain the possibility and imagine how I'd feel if it were to happen—a quiet house full of heavy sadness. My mother in her pajamas all day. No turkey or corn custard.

A flare of anger shoots through me. *I'm still here*, I think, *you have one kid left*.

"Maybe we'll go serve food at a soup kitchen," she says.

"I'll do whatever, but can we please just decide?" There's an edge to my voice that I don't want there, like a knife poking through even though I've tried wrapping it in a sheath of leather. "Please."

Selfie

On the Friday before she ended her life, Alexis took a selfie. In it, she wore a big pair of sunglasses and smiled. Her bonsai tree rested on the railing in the background. She and my father had been trying to nurse it back to health. I imagine her carrying the tree outside with her. I know that she would have talked to it in a sweet voice, telling it to enjoy the sun, calling it "little woobie" or something like that.

I've studied this picture, the last photo ever taken of my sister, studied her face and the things reflected in the lenses of her sunglasses, looking for clues. Sometimes it feels like if I look closely enough, I will come to some better sense of understanding about her death, but that hasn't happened. All I can see is that she does not look like someone who would be dead in less than twenty-four hours. She looks happy.

The Christmas Tree

"I TOLD DADDY no tree this year," my mother says to me on the phone. "We're not doing anything. Not decorating. Nothing."

It's an order, not a conversation, and it's typical of my mother. It's not, *I don't think I can handle a tree or decorations this year, honey, I just don't think I can do it.*

This is how my mother navigates her emotions. She does not explain her desires in relation to her feelings. She demands. She yells. I'm not sure whether she does this because she can't find the words, or whether she simply thinks that these things need no explanation.

My father appears to resent these declarations, despite the fact that he has long grown accustomed to them. Despite the fact that he loves my mother wholly and if she asked, he would, of course, be okay with no tree.

"Yeah, and after I told him," my mother says, referring to her no-tree declaration, "about a week later he said, 'Well, we're not getting a tree' in this sulky tone." There's a note of indignation in her voice, as if she couldn't imagine how he might possibly feel differently.

I can see clearly that my father wants a tree because he's desperate for normalcy. Desperate for the thrust of the tide of the cluttered world of his dead daughter to recede just an inch. It'll still be there, but maybe it won't wash all of their loose belongings away—flip-flops and plastic shovels dragged out to sea.

As I listen to all the details that my mother tells me, I weave together a narrative that explains how my father must be feeling. It's a thing I learned to do long ago. In my family, we rarely ask about one another's emotional state, but even when we do, we do not say how we really feel.

Instead, we say one thing but mean another; we say we are okay when we have been hurt by something, and then we expect the other party to play detective, to search for clues in our behavior that reflect our actual emotions, rather than our stated ones. This pattern of communication has been counterproductive to my ability to build intimacy in my relationships; I often find myself feeling not understood and lonely when Lindsay refuses to engage in the Sherlock Holmes role that I have grown accustomed to. I also find myself giving more weight to Lindsay's body language than I do to her words because words, in my experience, are nothing more than niceties. If you want to discern how another human is truly feeling, you must study them. This is the reason that I feel most seen by another human being when they figure out my internal state without me having to tell them.

It has taken real work to learn to say what I need and how I feel instead of how I think the other person wants me to feel, but I often default to the veiled manner of communicating, especially when I talk to either of my parents. We are so accustomed to searching for clues in tones of voice, in long pauses, in deep sighs. We tune in to the non-verbal cues and assign meaning to them.

And today on the phone with my mother is no different. From bits and pieces of information, I knit yet another square for the quilt full of assumptions that is the masterpiece of our family—a thing that we each add to, that each of us can hold up and study and analyze and react to, all without ever asking a single question.

A Father's Grief

On summer evenings, after hours of mowing, weeding, edging, sweeping, and fertilizing, my father would stand on the sidewalk in front of our house, sipping from a glass of ice water, condensation running down over his hand, broom leaning against his chest as he admired his lawn, which was the greenest, most well kept in the neighborhood.

Now, my father takes grass seed with him when he goes to visit Alexis's grave. I imagine him there, on his knees, sprinkling the seed, tending to that plot of land the way he did all those years ago—sweat on his brow, seeding the bare spots, then covering them with a sheet staked into the ground to protect against the birds.

The Rise and Fall of Yearning

ALEXIS COMES DOWNSTAIRS and finds her father asleep in the recliner. This has become his nightly ritual. He gets home from work, eats, changes out of his suit, and then plants himself here with a glass of red wine.

The soft glow from the flat-screen television casts moving shadows across his face. He snores arrhythmically with sudden stops and starts that nearly wake him. She watches his big belly rise and fall, rise and fall, and she thinks of how diminished he seems, even in spite of his newly acquired girth. He has gotten so big and he seems, always, so tired, though never too tired for work. He pours all of his energy there. Up at 5:30, out the door by 6:30, and not home until twelve hours later.

He's been this way for as long as she can remember. She cannot recall him ever taking a sick day, unlike his own father—a dentist—who was an alcoholic and a gambler. He doesn't talk much about his father, but once he told her about the way that his dad had made him send patients away when he was too hungover or too intoxicated to treat them. She's imagined him as a young child, shame burning on his face as he made excuses for his father's absence.

She walks to the pantry cabinet and opens the door, pulls out the bottle of red wine, gauges how much she can pour into her glass without anyone taking notice. When she was in high school, she did the same thing with their liquor. Occasionally, she'd add water to a bottle if she took too much. Anger flares inside of her at the fact that she's been reduced to sneaking alcohol. She is forty-one fucking years old, a fact she reminded her parents of just the other night. Old feelings have surfaced since she moved back home, rushing up like a float that was pushed to the bottom of a deep pool, then released. She is not a goddamn child.

This is supposed to be her home too, but she feels like an intruder. She has trained herself to do everything quietly—her steps have become soft shuffles, sshh sshh sounds as she moves across the hardwood floors; she sets glasses ever so gently on the granite counters—the gentlest ting; she doesn't even sing while she vacuums, which she absolutely loves to do. She senses this is what they want. When she talks to them at dinner they let out long sighs and exchange looks. Her mother rushes to change the subject, which is somewhat better than her father, who acts as if she hasn't spoken at all. Sitting at the counter every night where they eat dinner, she feels bulldozed. She never expected to feel so lonely around her parents.

She allows herself a half glass of wine. When she'd first moved in here, she drank their wine as she pleased, but eventually they restricted her. Told her that if she wanted to drink, she'd have to buy her own because she wasn't going to get looped every night drinking their alcohol. She'd rolled her eyes in response as if they were being petty and selfish, and said that was fine with her. Now she tags along with them when they go to the liquor store and buys her own when she can afford it.

She sips from her glass and stares out from the kitchen to where her father sleeps. She misses him, wishes she could hug him and bury her head into his shoulder. When she was a child, he called her "pumpkin" and carried her on his shoulders. She misses that and so many other things and people—their old house, her dead grandparents, her sister, the family's golden retriever, Lancelot. She yearns for things lost; lives in a perpetual state of grief and finds herself wondering how come other people seem better able to endure life's losses.

She has always been able to access her sad memories so much more readily than her happy ones. The happy ones existed somewhere inside, but they were buried under a thick layer of ice and she could only discern colors and patterns, no specifics. If you told her that her father taught her to ski, she would nod, with a tiny flicker of recognition, but she would not recall the way he gently held her up between his legs as they coasted down the bunny hill, the way he taught her to make a pie with her skis when she wanted to stop, the cups of hot cocoa they shared in the lodge sitting in front of the fire. If you reminded her how he beamed with pride when she graduated from college, she would know it was true, but she would not be able to recall his face, the tears welled in his eyes. What she would recall was the worry she'd carried that day that he was secretly disappointed because she graduated Magna, not Summa Cum Laude, as he had.

By contrast, her bad memories lived on top of the ice in the most vivid, vibrant colors. Crisp and clear, they slid all around her, swirling about. The time he called her stupid after she had let Danielle's hamster out of its cage and it crawled down the side of the radiator pipe and disappeared. The fights at the kitchen table over where she would go to college; the names both of her parents had called her—ingrate, selfish—the look in his eye the night he pushed his chair back from the table and grabbed her shoulders and shook her—all these instances were startlingly clear. When she thought of them, it felt like she was reliving them.

Her years of therapy have taught her to recognize the way that her brain worked, to understand that it's flawed, but this knowledge hasn't made it any easier to live, nor has she gained the ability to see things any other way. With each play of memories she feels like a piece of crumpled paper—a thing that will forever recall its creases, even after being smoothed out.

In the strangest way, she misses her dad's anger. Somewhere along the line he'd shut that down. She could barely get a reaction out of him these days. Instead, he presented himself as a picture of calm, but it was a calmness she suspected was born of apathy, of surrender, of hopelessness. She'd give anything to feel like he still cared.

Her mother is just the opposite, always exploding in anger and then apologizing later. Even though her words sometimes cut, they also bring small comfort because they reveal that she hasn't yet given up on her. On more than a handful of nights, her mother has curled her body next to hers and held her until the morning.

How could this be her life? She looks once again at her father, his long nose, his five o'clock shadow, his thinning grey hair. Both her mother and father are pushing seventy. When they die, she will be alone. Dani wants nothing to do with her. She thinks of the difference between being lonely in the company of loved ones and being alone, and wonders which is worse. She finishes her wine and returns to the pantry for more. *Fuck it*, she thinks, and fills her glass to the top before returning to her small bedroom.

The Tenses of Loss

AT MY SUPPORT group, I am deferential to the parents who lost a child. In the grief hierarchy, they're at the top. This feels like a universally known and agreed-upon fact. But this month, a woman whom I've grown fond of for her insightful, sensitive comments makes this unspoken truth explicit when she reveals that, in addition to losing her son, she also lost a brother to suicide years ago. "It's just not the same," she tells the group. "They say that when you lose your parents, you lose your past; when you lose your sibling, you lose your present; when you lose a child, you lose your future."

Hearing this only confirms the feeling I sometimes have when I'm here that my grief is small in comparison to others. I think of my parents. Do they feel their future is gone? I think of this woman's son, just sixteen, handsome with red hair, and then of the woman and her husband finding their son's body, still warm. How the warmth probably destroys them anew every day with its *almost*, its *not-quite*.

I see myself squished in at the very bottom of the grief hierarchy, elbowing my way in, like a child desperate to not be the last in line. I lost a sister I rarely liked; a sister I tried, but mostly failed, to love. If I didn't love her when she was here, who the hell am I to mourn her when she is gone?

After the meeting, the woman catches up with me as I walk to my car. "I hope you didn't feel that I was dismissing your loss with what I said, because that's not what I meant to do. It's just that the two losses were so different for me."

"No no," I say. "I understood what you meant."

And while this is true, if I were being completely honest, I would tell her about all of the questions that flooded my brain in response to her words. I would tell her that the things she said solidified the judgments I already carried toward my grief. But I am not being honest. I am walking to my car with a woman who has lived through finding her dead son. I will not dare add one burden to her load. Instead, I tell her that Lindsay is pregnant and that I am beginning to understand the fact that the love a parent has for a child is different from any other love. This is also true.

"Ooh, I am so happy for you," she says sincerely. "Congratulations."

"Thanks," I say. "I'm really excited."

I think of Lindsay at home in bed, four months pregnant. I remember the moment we found out that she was pregnant and the way that in that moment all of our focus shifted from the present to the future, to what would be, to what kind of moms we would be. I know this woman is right. A child is a future.

Two Losses

AT MY GRIEF group, people talk about Anthony Bourdain and Kate Spade's suicides.

"Maybe this will help reduce the stigma," one woman says. "I mean, even these people who seem to have everything going for them, when they end their lives, it's like, c'mon, depression is a disease."

"I'm upset at the way the media reported on it," another woman interjects. "They have to tell every little detail. They even told the color of the scarf that Kate Spade used." She shakes her head in disgust.

I want to add another viewpoint—to defend the public's curiosity because it seems like the most natural thing in the world to me. Even when death comes to someone in the most benign way, people ask questions about the circumstances: who found them, how long had they been dead, what caused it. People yearn for understanding.

Besides, why does it matter if people know whether the scarf was red or blue or green anyway? Dead is dead, and if the whole world knows how it happened there is no shame in that, no shame in saying that your loved one took pills or stabbed themselves or wrapped a noose around their neck or pulled a trigger or slit a wrist. It all leads to the same place. The only thing that seems a shame to me is the fact that there are so many people who choose to die because living is too painful.

Practice Breaths

Because Lindsay is of "advanced maternal age," once she reaches thirty-six weeks, she has to go for twice-weekly sonograms to monitor things like the level of her amniotic fluid. Mostly these visits are routine and uneventful, but today we are watching to see if the fetus is taking practice breaths—a developmental milestone that sets the baby up for success in taking its first breaths outside of the womb.

"Now we might not see any and that's okay," the tech says to both of us before we start the appointment. "We'll be watching for them as we move forward, but sometimes we just don't catch them right away. If we don't see them today, it's not something to necessarily worry about just yet."

I hear what the tech is saying, but I don't believe her. It feels like a pretty high-stakes visit and I know that if we leave here without seeing a practice breath, I will be telling myself over and over not to worry "just yet," which is only a thing that people tell themselves when they are clearly already worried.

The technician slathers Lindsay's large belly with warmed

clear gel and moves a wand over it. A familiar, grainy image appears on the screen and the tech takes down measurements as we stare, transfixed. His head is larger than average, and we both laugh at this news because this is a trait that Lindsay and many of her family members have. Lindsay can never find hats big enough to fit her head.

Lindsay and I know we are having a boy, but we've kept this knowledge secret from everyone. This was the compromise we reached when we disagreed about finding out the sex. Lindsay didn't think she could make it without knowing the sex, but I wanted it to be a surprise.

"What if we find out, but we keep it to ourselves?" I'd asked. "I just don't want all of these gendered gifts." What I'd really meant was that I didn't want a bunch of pink clothes and blankets because I was planning on being the kind of parent who had awareness of gender stereotypes and tried my best not to pass them along. Whether we were having a boy or a girl, I wanted them to have equal access to both trucks and dolls, dinosaurs and tea sets, blue and pink.

"Okay," Lindsay had agreed. "I can do that." The secret was nice. It felt like a warm ball that we passed back and forth between one another. When people proclaimed with certainty that they thought it was a boy or a girl, we just nodded and gave each other the side eye.

"Well," the tech says, "it looks like he's asleep in there. I'm going to try to wake him up," she says before pushing on Lindsay's belly. He shimmies around a bit in response to her gyrations.

Each time we have an ultrasound of our child, I feel a sense of both confirmation and disbelief. When I see this being before me—arms, legs, fingers—and I hear the heartbeat, I know that it's real, but there's part of me that cannot comprehend that this being is our child. It's a truth that feels too big and unwieldy to hold. I feel much the same about

Alexis's death—a knowing mixed with an inability to grasp. Sure, she is dead, but how could it be that she's dead forever?

"Oh yeah, he's awake now," the tech says. I let out a delighted squeak as he begins shifting around. "Okay, you're going to want to look here," the tech says, pointing to his lungs.

I stare and stare, willing something to happen. *Breathe*, I think, *please breathe*. I stare so hard that my eyes lose focus. On one of our earlier ultrasounds, they showed us a 3-D view, but I'd recoiled when I'd seen it.

"I did not like that 3-D one," I'd said to Lindsay later. "It looked like an alien."

Lindsay had laughed. "Yeah, it was kind of creepy."

The tech inhales sharply. "There it is," she says excitedly. I refocus on the screen and see what she sees. A series of four or five shuddering movements near the lungs. Our child is inside of Lindsay and he is practicing breathing. He is getting ready to transition out of the fluid, protected world of the womb. He's preparing in there in the same way that we have been getting ready out here.

The Every Child

WHEN MY SON, Cooper, is born, the grief does not leave my body. As it turns out, my body is capable of holding joy and grief. They act together on me like nothing I've ever known. They do not war inside of me or fight over territory. They are cooperative, polite. *Hello,* they say to one another, *please make yourself at home. Can I take your coat? Get you something to drink?* They blend together and then separate. They take turns rising up while the other recedes. I am exuberant one minute, tearful the next.

When I first see Cooper, I know so many things in an instant that I had no clue about before he was born. I know a new kind of love, one that is fierce, vigilant, ready to destroy anything that threatens. I know an urge to protect, to wrap my body around his and shield him from every bad thing in the world. I know the deepest flicker of fear that this boy could disappear just as mysteriously as he appeared. Most of all, I know that my parents will never forgive themselves for not saving Alexis, even though the sin of losing her was not theirs. This is a parents' burden, one that I now share.

I look and look at my beautiful boy when he is born, at his tiny fingers fully formed, at his fingernails that already need to be trimmed, at his ears. How can it be that he grew from nothing into this? How can it be that he was inside of Lindsay for all these months? How can he exist? The wonder is so powerful that it feels as though it's uniquely mine, but surely this emotion belongs to every new parent. And surely, it belonged to my mother and father when they first held Alexis in their arms.

This thought is a revelation that cleaves—uniting me with them just as it separates. I understand what they've lost, but I hope to never understand.

Journals

EVEN THOUGH I'VE talked with my therapist about reading Alexis's journals, it worries Lindsay.

"It's just something I need to do," I tell her. "I don't know how else to explain it."

"Okay," she says, but she looks wary.

"I'm being very deliberate about which ones I choose," I say. "I haven't let myself read any of the more recent ones, because I'm not ready." I hope that this will make her feel better, but she doesn't look convinced. "I'm taking care of myself," I assure her, but she only nods.

My mother has all of Alexis's journals, twenty or thirty books, in an ornate chest in the basement of their home. Each time I go to visit, I stuff a couple into my bag and bring them back with me and then devour them.

When I crack one open before bed, I can feel Lindsay's fear come to life, like a pinwheel in the breeze, quietly whirring. What I don't tell Lindsay is that I am afraid too, afraid to read a line that I will never be able to forget—that Alexis hated me or that she killed herself because I didn't love her.

But I've decided the earliest journals are safe. They begin when she was ten years old, and they're full of daily entries about which boy she likes and who's her best friend. The best friends shift almost as quickly as the boys she has crushes on—one day it's Pat from her baseball team, the next Brett from school, the next Henry Thomas, the star of *E.T.*, then Todd who she writes is "the perfect match" for her except that he is "only in a book." "I'm looking for my real life Todd," she writes.

As I read, my guard drops. I feel like I am meeting my sister all over again, rediscovering the silly, overly dramatic, dreamy person I'd lost to her illnesses. She signs the entries with different names: "Kitty" and then "Hot Shot" and then back to "Kitty" before changing again to "Princess Gloria," which she shortens to "P.G.," then it's "Loni" for a couple of months, and then "Capricorn" until she finally settles on "Eden."

For a while, under each entry, she writes her emotional state in parentheses. Most common among these is "confused," but she also peppers in "angrily speechless," "happy and scared," "hot and sweaty," "thoughtful and satisfied," "proud and elated," and "freshly in love." I often find myself laughing out loud. Sometimes she writes in code or Pig Latin because her annoying little sister has been reading her diary.

For the most part, all of the entries are light and airy, full of hilarious declarations about how she is opening a restaurant called the "Shady Lady Café" in our basement and how she plans to try out for tennis in the '88 Olympics. This entry is immediately followed by another where she confesses that she is terrible at tennis, but insists that she still plans on trying out for the Olympics. In one, she reports gloomily that her singing career is over, but she doesn't explain why.

Amidst all of the funny subjects that Alexis writes about, I see the underpinnings of her mental illness—shadowy blurs that someone else might brush off as the ups and downs of adolescence, but I know they are more than that. I see them as emotional extremes, a thin thread woven into her personality that became coarser over time.

After about a year of making careful and deliberate choices around which journal to read next, on one visit home I pick up the very last one she ever kept. I'm not ready for it, but something in me decides that I need to see whatever ugliness it holds because ever since Cooper was born, it feels like I have papered over the pain around Alexis. I've been so busy tending to my son and all the accompanying emotions that have swelled in me since his birth that some days it feels like I've cordoned off my grief into a small room and I've shut the door. Some days, my sister feels like a shadow memory. I know that reading this journal will be like running a blade across my skin, the way that she used to, but I am hungry for the pain. *Maybe we are not so different*, I think, *maybe I need to make myself bleed to know that I'm still alive.*

I open the journal. Alexis's handwriting is unfamiliar, pointier and smaller, and not at all like the loopy, bubbly writing in the old letters we sent to each other, which we signed every time with "Love Always." She writes about her hallucinations, which I learn were both auditory and visual. There's mention of a clown appearing in the corner of her room and of a night when she was so afraid that people were going to come out of her closet that she rigged up some sort of lock on the door. There are lists of medications scribbled with amounts next to them, as well as amounts of alcohol. These lists are followed by notes about how loud or quiet the voices in her head became in response to these doses.

I feel things collapse inside of me.

There are notes about different illnesses that she researched as she tried to figure out what was causing her hallucinations: partial complex seizures and sleep states are two of the things noted. There are entries about a bidding war that she got into with another person on eBay. She writes about how "the bitch" keeps outbidding her. Pages later, she makes the discovery that "the bitch" she's been bidding against was herself—that she'd created another eBay account that she had no recollection of.

She must have been so frightened. I think of how cold I was to her—of the times I rolled my eyes on the other end of the phone line when she complained, of the thank-you call I refused to make to her for the wedding present she sent to Lindsay and I even though she couldn't really afford one.

I have failed to die 13 times, she writes at one point.

This flattens me. Anything that was left standing inside of me just falls.

I close the book and sit wondering how she survived as long as she did.

The Requirement of Grief

AS TIME PASSES, I learn that grief's only requirement is that it must be carried. It does not care if you are ready for it or if its weight is too much to bear or if you are in the throes of the deepest joy.

It cannot be set aside even for the briefest moment while you sit on a park bench and enjoy a beautiful sunset. Even then, it must be carried. Carried even as you watch in wonder on the day your son comes into the world. Carried when you bear witness to your parents holding their only grandchild for the very first time. Carried always.

Anniversary

ON THE TWO-YEAR anniversary of Alexis's death, I hike on a trail near where she attended her first rehab. I tell Lindsay that I am planning to take the day off of work, and ask her if she can pick Cooper up from daycare even though it's my day. She waves her hand in the air and says, "Of course. Just let me know where you're planning to be in case you get lost or something."

"I'll be fine," I say. "I can follow the trail markers."

She stares at me for a moment as if contemplating something, then says gently, "D, you have no sense of direction. I'd just like to know where you are."

I nod in acknowledgment, knowing that she's right. It had only been in recent years that I'd begun relying on a GPS and had stopped getting hopelessly lost on trips to nearby places that I should have been able to navigate on my own.

Last year on the first anniversary, I drove to Philly to be with my parents. We went to church and then to the cemetery to visit Alexis's grave. This year, I want to be alone. I want to walk. To walk so much that I hurt my body, make it ache, so that when I wake up tomorrow I'll be reminded of today by the weariness in my bones.

Our parents have been married for forty-eight years today. I wonder again whether Alexis meant to share their anniversary. I don't know how to deal with these two events falling on the same day, so I text my parents, saying just that.

I walk for almost ten miles, looking at the trees, watching my feet step over stones, rising to avoid getting caught on a root. Is this a way for me to affirm my ableness? That I am continuing on? Is this a giant "fuck you" to my sister—a way of saying "look at me, doing the things you couldn't?" Or am I walking in honor of her, *because* she couldn't? I don't know. But I don't lose my footing once. I don't stumble or fall or shed one tear. I don't know whether I'm healed or made of tin.

The Final Product

EVEN THOUGH I am present for all of the back-and-forth deliberations over the tombstone, I am stunned a few months later when I get an email from my mother with the subject line: *What do you think?* I open it to find a photo of the stone they've chosen.

It's polished black with a cross and a butterfly engraved on it, and a quote from Emerson on the side. The top bears our family name and beneath it, *Alexis V.* is etched with my sister's date of birth and death dashed out. Her name is flanked by the names of my parents: *Clare and Nicholas W.,* along with their respective years of birth. All that's missing is the date of their deaths.

I hate it more than I've ever hated anything in my life.

I type my reply and hit send: *Looks as nice as any tombstone with your names on it could.*

Side by Side

In the spring of 2019, Alexis has been gone for nearly three years. Since she died, each spring has been particularly harrowing for me. The memory of her loss leans up against the majesty of new life blooming all around me and tinges it with sadness. Although I no longer curse the grass for growing or the birds for building their nests, as I did that first spring without her, I still cannot witness all the newness without thinking of her death. When I go outside and see that the daffodils have pushed up out of the earth, that the neighbor's forsythia bush is full of yellow flowers, and that the magnolias are readying themselves for a masterful display, I remember her.

Cooper is almost two years old. He was born a little over one year after Alexis died, and the two of them will always be linked through this time gap. When he turns three, Alexis will be dead for four years. The older he gets, the further away she will be. These two things create a tension: joy pressing up against sadness.

"Do you want oatmeal for breakfast?" I ask Cooper on

one of these beautiful spring mornings. In the past month or two his language has exploded. He's beginning to put words together to make sentences and I am fascinated by it. I recall the way Alexis read to me and taught me the meaning of new words.

"Yes and no," he says.

"Yes, you want oatmeal?" I ask, laughing, trying to convey that these two words cancel one another out; cannot exist side by side. "Or no, you don't want oatmeal?"

"Yes and no," he says again, as if he knows better than me. He runs to the other room to play with his barn.

I watch his small frame disappear around the wall, and it strikes me that yes and no fit perfectly together into this new life of mine, the one that opened up after Alexis died and Cooper was born. The two truths of my life—that he is alive and that she is dead—live side by side in me. Being alive requires that I hold my deepest sorrow alongside my greatest joy; hold them in my palm and let them swirl together. They are mine to carry with me, always, and I do not need to separate them, to worry about one taking something away from the other.

As I stand in the kitchen with an oatmeal packet in my hand, listening to my son make animal sounds from the living room, I am filled with gratitude for Alexis and Cooper. They are my two greatest teachers. Alexis's death has shaped me into a hollowed-out vessel, ready to receive all of the lessons that Cooper will pour into me, for as long as I have him.

Yes and no.

Yes and no.

Yes and no.

Acknowledgments

A book going out into the world is not a singular affair, and this one is no different. There are so many hands that have touched the pages, so many eyes that have read and reread, and so many who have cared for me while I wrote, or who have cared for my writing.

I'd like to thank my mother and father for reading this manuscript and generously giving me their feedback. You had a lot of notes and questions, and I want you to know that I received each one as a radical act of love that you doled out with grace and kindness. I know it was beyond difficult to read what I'd written. I realize that having a daughter who writes creative nonfiction is not always a joyous experience. Thanks for not disowning me.

This book wouldn't exist without Judith Krummeck, the one and only remaining member of a writing group that was started many years ago. I don't know how I ever got lucky enough to have you as my partner, but your insights are invaluable, your questions are challenging, and you push me toward excellence, while also encouraging me to be myself.

Thank you for the countless hours you pored over this and helped to shape it. Thank you for believing in me enough not to sugarcoat your feedback when my writing was shitty. Thank you for FaceTiming through the pandemic, and then when it was warm enough, for sitting outside by the stream in a fold-up chair with a laptop perched on your lap. Can't wait for our next "writing group."

To my friend and mentor, Marion Winik, who read and gave me her real and raw responses to this manuscript and who also invited me over to enjoy a dinner that she cooked while we discussed each of her comments. This book would not be the same without your keen eye, and I would not be the writer I am without your many hours of guidance.

Thanks to the Rehoboth Beach Writers Guild, especially Maribeth Fisher. When I signed up to take a class with the guild many years ago, I was lucky enough to get Maribeth as my teacher. It was under her tutelage that I began writing this book. At the time I didn't know that's what I was doing, but Maribeth did, and she kept telling me every chance she got. I didn't believe her, but it turned out she was right.

Many thanks to Art Farm and Soaring Gardens, the two residencies I attended while working on this manuscript. Ed Dadey of Art Farm has created the weirdest, wildest place artists can go to be who they are without restraint, and I appreciate his vision. I am equally grateful to the Ora Lerman Trust, which funds the Soaring Gardens Writing Residency. Soaring Gardens allowed me to be quiet and alone, and forced me to face some very difficult fears.

Thanks to Tammy Letherer, my editor, who helped me see all the ways that *I* was missing from my own memoir. Your insights were invaluable.

Much gratitude to my amazing wife Lindsay. You have always generously encouraged me to write my truth even when you know that reading it might make you uncomfortable. Thank you for seeing me, knowing me, and giving me the time and space for my art. Your understanding allows me to pursue the thing that brings me the most peace. I don't know who I would be without that freedom, and I am lucky that you know this about me.

And last, thank you to my sister Alexis and my son Cooper. Being given the opportunity to be a sister and a mother are two of the greatest honors I will ever know. Thank you for the lessons you've taught me and all the ones that lie ahead.

About the Author

DANIELLE ARIANO received her MFA in Creative Nonfiction from the University of Baltimore. As part of her thesis, she wrote, designed, and published her first book, *Getting Over the Rainbow*, a memoir recounting her humorous and sometimes painful experiences coming out as a lesbian.

Ariano's work has been published in *Salon*, *Huff Post*, *Baltimore City Paper*, *Baltimore Fishbowl*, *North Dakota Quarterly*, *Cobalt Review*, and *Welter*. She is a former columnist for *Baltimore Gay Life*, and she has been featured on WYPR's radio show, *The Signal*.

When she is not writing, Ariano works as a cabinetmaker. She has great reverence for the hallowed, dusty smell of a woodshop. She lives in Lutherville, Maryland, with her wife, son, and dog. Visit her website at www.danielleariano.com.

www.ingramcontent.com/pod-product-compliance
Lightning Source LLC
Chambersburg PA
CBHW020905160726
47993CB00005B/1829